Discover Orlando, Florida

Your Ultimate Travel and Vacation Guide

R. T. Kagels

© Copyright 2023 - All rights reserved.

The content contained within this book may not be reproduced, duplicated or transmitted without direct written permission from the author or the publisher.

Under no circumstances will any blame or legal responsibility be held against the publisher, or author, for any damages, reparation, or monetary loss due to the information contained within this book, either directly or indirectly.

Legal Notice:

This book is copyright protected. It is only for personal use. You cannot amend, distribute, sell, use, quote or paraphrase any part, or the content within this book, without the consent of the author or publisher.

Disclaimer Notice:

Please note the information contained within this document is for educational and entertainment purposes only. All effort has been executed to present accurate, up to date, reliable, complete information. No warranties of any kind are declared or implied. Readers acknowledge that the author is not engaged in the rendering of legal, financial, medical or professional advice. The content within this book has been derived from various sources. Please consult a licensed professional before attempting any techniques outlined in this book.

By reading this document, the reader agrees that under no circumstances is the author responsible for any losses, direct or indirect, that are incurred as a result of the use of the information contained within this document, including, but not limited to, errors, omissions, or inaccuracies.

Table of Contents

INTRODUCTION 1

CHAPTER 1: ORLANDO UNVEILED—A CITY OVERVIEW 5
   THE HISTORY AND GROWTH OF ORLANDO 5
   ORLANDO'S DIVERSE NEIGHBORHOODS 8
      Downtown Districts: A Vibrant Core 9
      Hidden Gems and Lesser-Known Areas 10
   ORLANDO'S YEAR-ROUND CLIMATE AND EVENTS 12
   DID YOU KNOW? 15
   SHARE YOUR INSIGHTS! 15
   TIME TO GET PACKING! 17

CHAPTER 2: PLANNING YOUR TRIP 19
   WHEN TO VISIT 20
   TRANSPORTATION AROUND ORLANDO 25
   WHERE TO STAY 28
      Types of Accommodations 29
      Different Options For All Kinds of Travelers 29
   HOW MUCH MONEY TO BUDGET FOR YOUR TRIP 33
   DID YOU KNOW? 35
   SHARE YOUR INSIGHTS! 36
   YOU'RE ALMOST THERE 36

CHAPTER 3: THE MAGIC OF THEME PARKS 39
   WALT DISNEY WORLD 39
   UNIVERSAL ORLANDO 41
   OTHER THEME PARKS AND ATTRACTIONS 43
      SeaWorld Orlando and Aquatica Park 43
      LEGOLAND Florida Resort 45
      Gatorland 45
      Fun Spot America 46
   DID YOU KNOW? 47
   SHARE YOUR INSIGHTS! 48
   ONCE YOU'VE HAD YOUR FILL OF ACTION, HOW ABOUT A CHANGE OF PACE? 49

CHAPTER 4: NATURE TIME IN ORLANDO 51

PARKS AND NATURE SPOTS 52
The Everglades: A Natural Marvel 52
Wekiwa Springs: A Local Gem 53
Other Nature Parks and Areas Near Orlando 54
Bird-Watching in Orlando 55
FUN NATURE TOURS 57
Boat Tours Near Orlando 57
Kayaking Near Orlando 58
Animal Encounters 60
WALKS AND BIKE RIDES 64
Trails 64
DID YOU KNOW? 68
SHARE YOUR INSIGHTS! 68
ARE YOU HUNGRY YET? 69

CHAPTER 5: RESTAURANTS AND FOOD 71

MUST-TRY FOODS 72
International Drive: A World of Flavors 72
STANDOUT RESTAURANTS NEAR INTERNATIONAL DRIVE 74
American Classics and International Fusion 74
Latin American Specialties 76
European Cuisine 79
Asian Fare 80
The Seafood Scene 81
Sweet Treats Galore 84
IN-PARK FOOD OPTIONS 85
UNIQUE MEALS IN THE MAGIC KINGDOM AND BEYOND 86
Character-Themed Dishes 86
EATING ON A BUDGET IN THE MAGIC KINGDOM AND UNIVERSAL STUDIOS 86
Budget-Friendly Tips 86
FOOD EVENTS 88
Epcot International Food and Wine Festival 88
Fall Food Festivals 89
FOOD TRUCKS IN THE CITY BEAUTIFUL 90
World Food Truck Park in Kissimmee 90
DID YOU KNOW? 92
SHARE YOUR INSIGHTS! 92
READY FOR MORE ACTIVITIES YET? LET'S GO! 93

CHAPTER 6: FAMILY FUN TIME 95

PARKS FOR KIDS 95
LEARN AND PLAY 97
   Science *98*
   Art and History *100*
   Animal Encounters *101*
MORE FUN IDEAS 104
DID YOU KNOW? 105
SHARE YOUR INSIGHTS! 106
SICK OF THE KIDS YET? IT'S DATE NIGHT TIME! 107

CHAPTER 7: LOVE IN ORLANDO 109

DINNER DATES 110
   Candlelight Charm *110*
   Lake and Riverside Views *112*
COUPLES ACTIVITIES 113
WHERE TO STAY 115
DID YOU KNOW? 118
SHARE YOUR INSIGHTS! 119
FOR ALL YOU SOLO TRAVELERS OUT THERE: DON'T FRET 119

CHAPTER 8: SOLO TIME IN ORLANDO 121

DO IT YOUR WAY 121
CULTURE STOPS 124
STAY SAFE AND HAPPY 127
DID YOU KNOW? 128
SHARE YOUR INSIGHTS! 129
THINK YOU'VE SEEN IT ALL YET? 130

CHAPTER 9: DAY TRIPS 131

NEAR THE OCEAN 131
   Beaches *132*
   Serene Seaside Towns *133*
NATURE-ORIENTED DAY TRIPS 134
CULTURAL DAY TRIPS 136
DID YOU KNOW? 138
SHARE YOUR INSIGHTS! 139
I'VE GOT A SECRET FOR YOU 140

CHAPTER 10: AN INSIDER'S GUIDE 141

ODD AND FUN SPOTS 141
LOCAL FAVORITES 146

Farmer's Markets *146*
Orlando's Craft Breweries *148*
SMOOTH TRIP TIPS 149
DID YOU KNOW? 152
SHARE YOUR INSIGHTS! 153
BIDDING FAREWELL TO "THE CITY BEAUTIFUL" 153

BONUS CHAPTER: OFF THE BEATEN PATH **155**

ORLANDO'S HIDDEN FLAVORS 155
SPEAKEASIES AND DIVES 156
Speakeasies *156*
Dive Bars *157*
SPOOKY FUN IN THE CITY BEAUTIFUL 157
SHARE YOUR INSIGHTS! 158

CONCLUSION **161**

AUTHOR BIOGRAPHY **163**

REFERENCES **165**

IMAGE REFERENCES 202

Introduction

Orlando: It's a name that so many of us associate with fun, one that conjures images of enchantment and adventure. Images of Mouseketeer-hatted throngs of happy vacationers flash before our eyes; we can almost see fireworks bursting over the spires of the Magic Kingdom and can almost feel the thrill of riding one of Universal Studios' epic rollercoasters.

But that's not all. It's also about the palm trees and the beaches of the Space Coast, which are just a short car ride away. We can almost smell the sunscreen as the smell of piña coladas wafts over us, activating our imaginary senses. *Ahhhhh, paradise!* We think to ourselves. This is what artists like the Beach Boys and Jimmy Buffet were singing about the promise of a tropical vacation that's always just beyond our grasp. Well, I'm here to tell you that It'll be beyond your grasp no more!

That's right! While going on vacation anywhere across the fifty-nifty can cost an arm and a leg, it doesn't have to. For many, Orlando is a destination steeped in whimsy, a place where fantasy and reality collide and where your wallet ends up empty after making the family's dreams come true. But it doesn't have to be this way! In these pages, we're going to unveil a different side of Orlando, one you may not have expected and one that'll allow you to have a great time no matter what your budget.

In this book, I'm going to whisk you away to a world where Orlando is much more than just theme parks, attractions, and rides. Our adventure begins with a story, one that many of you can relate to. It's a tale of discovery, shared experiences, and the pursuit of something extraordinary.

In a remote corner of Orlando, away from all the crowds, I one day found myself sitting in a cafe with my 76-year-old mother. Her zest for life and love for exploration were my inspiration for planning the trip together. As we explored the city's lesser-known gems and charming neighborhoods, I realized that Orlando held a secret side that most visitors never uncover. As a lifelong Florida resident, even I was blind to what I discovered.

But the story didn't end there. When I got back home, I reached out to fellow travelers, like my good friends Barry and Gail, fellow Orlando enthusiasts who shared their own Orlando vacation stories. Their experiences were also vibrant, real, and filled with insights that can't be found in ordinary guidebooks.

You see, I understand the challenges you face as a traveler. The overwhelming information, the generic recommendations, and the desire for something unique. That's why I've written this book. The catalyst that brought you here might be a longing for adventure, a quest for the undiscovered, or simply a desire to escape the ordinary. Whatever it is, I understand it, and that's why I've written this book, giving you instant access to insiders' secrets.

So, what exactly can you expect within the pages of this guide? Allow me to share a glimpse of what you'll have access to:

- **expert guidance**: This book is filled to the brim with well-researched insider tips on getting the most out of your Orlando adventure. There's absolutely no need to spend hours scouring the internet—it's all here at your fingertips.

- **save money**: I'll show you how to enjoy Orlando without breaking the bank. From budget meals to special deals and off-peak travel, your wallet will thank you.

- **a plan that works for everyone**: Whether you're traveling solo, with a loved one, or with the whole family, there are a multitude of itinerary options to fit your unique travel style and needs.

- **hidden gems**: Beyond the well-known attractions, you'll get to know some of the less-crowded spots and activities for an experience that's truly one-of-a-kind.

- **time savers**: I'll be sharing exclusive pro tips with you so you can spend more time enjoying your trip and less time planning it.

But don't just take my word for it. This book has already earned its stripes in its exclusive pre-press version, and readers have spoken and passed me their feedback. Their stories, some of which will be shared in this book, serve as testimonials, real experiences that have shaped their own Orlando adventures. The insights of these seasoned travelers will help paint a vivid picture of what awaits you on your magical Orlando getaway.

Now, you might be wondering, who am I to guide you through Orlando? Well, I'm your fellow explorer, your Orlando enthusiast—my friends just call me R.T. During all my time in the Sunshine State, I've lived and breathed this city, discovering its many secrets, and my passion is sharing them with you. Together, we'll explore the exciting places, tips, and secrets revealed through these chapters, each filled with the promise of a better, more vibrant Orlando experience.

So, whether you're an Orlando newcomer or a seasoned visitor looking for something beyond the ordinary, this book can serve as your guide to a city of endless possibilities in what we call "The City Beautiful." It's time to flip the script and experience Orlando like a local. Buckle up—our adventure is just beginning.

If you're wondering whether this is the right book for you, *yes, it is!* And Orlando *is* the right destination. So, let's get going already!

Chapter 1:

Orlando Unveiled—A City Overview

Who would've thought? Did you know that Orlando has a history that goes way beyond its reputation as the "Theme Park Capital of the World?" Well, it does! The city has a rich history that's just as interesting as the thrills and adventures that we often associate with it. To truly appreciate this vibrant city, we need to step back in time and explore its roots.

The History and Growth of Orlando

Though it was originally inhabited by the Timucua and Seminole tribes, Orlando's modern-day story begins in 1838. It was originally established as a military outpost called Fort Gatlin, located just south of present-day Orlando city limits. During this time, settlers were under heavy attack by Native Americans as the Seminole Wars raged on. The original name of the community surrounding the fort was Jernigan, taking the surname of the family that helped establish the first settlement outside the fort.

It wasn't until 1856 that the area officially received its modern-day name, and the local post office changed the official name the following year. Some say the name came from Orlando Reeves, a U.S. Army lookout man who was killed during these conflicts after spotting a floating log while on his watchman duties. It turned out this log was a trojan horse of sorts; though Reeves shot at it, his life was swiftly taken in a hail of flying arrows launched by the Native attackers.

There are at least three other versions of how the name "Orlando" came to be, two involving a local judge named James Speer, who had an affinity for Shakespeare, and another involving a guy who was, in fact, named Orlando who was driving a herd of oxen through the area. No matter what the origin of the name, the city of Orlando was finally incorporated in 1875.

As Orlando grew, it became an agricultural center and was an important place for cotton and livestock up until the Civil War. After the Union won the war, much of the South was devastated and left in economic shambles. Orlando again became an important place for agriculture, this time, however, for oranges and other citrus fruits.

The end of the 19th century saw the arrival of the steam rail, and for the first time, people could actually get to Central Florida with ease. Soon enough, the rail line was also extended to Tampa, connecting Orlando with Florida's Gulf Coast.

Growth really started to pick up in the region around the mid-20th Century. The opening of the Cape Canaveral Aerospace Center was instrumental in this growth, as it brought jobs and economic opportunity to the region. It was at this time that population density began to increase, and a burgeoning tourism market would soon fuel further growth. Commercial passenger flights were still prohibitively expensive at the time, and most

Americans still vacationed by car on the country's newly paved interstate highway system.

Whatever way people were getting to Florida, the writing was on the wall: the uptick in tourism represented a huge market, and the Walt Disney Company saw a huge opportunity in Orlando and the booming tourism that was rippling across the Sunshine State.

In 1971, Walt Disney World Resort opened its doors, marking the birth of the modern Orlando that we know today. This event catapulted Orlando into the global spotlight and brought about an influx of tourists.

But it's not just Walt Disney World that reshaped the city. Over the years, numerous other theme parks, including Universal Orlando Resort and SeaWorld, have joined the landscape. These attractions turned Orlando into a destination that countless American families dreamed of, offering not just amusement and entertainment but also immersive experiences that have proven capable of captivating the hearts of millions.

Beyond its status as a tourist hub, today's Orlando has evolved into a multifaceted city boasting a number of diverse industries. While tourism is undeniably a major player, Orlando is also a thriving center for technology, aerospace, and healthcare.

NASA's Kennedy Space Center, the launch center for Cape Canaveral is, of course, still a major presence that's felt throughout the region. But that's not all for science and engineering in the region, as there's also the Medical City complex in Lake Nona, which has become a hub for medical research and innovation.

Orlando's growth goes hand in hand with its cultural diversity and thriving communities. Today, it's a place where a world of international cultures work, play, and enjoy life, and the city boasts a diverse range of neighborhoods, each one telling a unique story about its residents.

As you explore the city further, you'll discover hidden gems beyond the theme parks. Whether it's the buzzing culinary scene, the vibrant arts and music culture, or the numerous recreational opportunities in its many lakes and parks, Orlando is a city that represents a myriad of experiences and possibilities and, moreover, is a city of imagination!

Now that we've painted a picture of Orlando's history let's take a closer look at the city's neighborhoods, climate, and annual festivals and events to start getting a better picture of what this extraordinary city is really all about. Orlando's story is far from over; rather, it stands today as an ever-evolving dynamic collection of experiences just waiting to be discovered!

Orlando's Diverse Neighborhoods

To truly grasp the essence of Orlando, it's essential to explore its eclectic neighborhoods, each offering a unique slice of this multifaceted city. From bustling downtown areas to hidden gems in the outskirts, all of Orlando's neighborhoods have stories to tell.

Downtown Districts: A Vibrant Core

The heart of Orlando is its downtown districts, which collectively make for a lively and dynamic urban core. When visiting, keep an eye out for these key areas:

- **Downtown Orlando:** The epicenter of the city, Downtown Orlando is home to skyscrapers, theaters, and a thriving nightlife scene. Church Street Station is known for its entertainment, while Lake Eola Park provides a tranquil escape in the midst of the city's hustle and bustle.

- **City District-Main Street:** A bustling hub of restaurants, bars, and boutiques, City District-Main Street offers a taste of Orlando's local culture. The historic charm and variety of dining options make it a must-visit.

- **Thornton Park:** Nestled just east of Downtown, this charming neighborhood is known for its cobblestone streets, boutique shops, and picturesque bungalows. Stroll along the brick-lined streets and enjoy the local dining scene.

- **Winter Park:** A picturesque enclave, the area is renowned for its beautiful parks, boutique shopping, and the stunning Rollins College campus. Take a boat tour along the tranquil Chain of Lakes, or explore the Morse Museum, home to the largest collection of famed art nouveau designer Louis Comfort Tiffany's works.

Hidden Gems and Lesser-Known Areas

Orlando's real charm often lies in its lesser-explored neighborhoods, cherished by locals and often missed by tourists. Here are a few hidden gems to discover:

- **Mills 50 District:** An area brimming with diverse culture, this area is known for its culinary scene. Enjoy international cuisine, art galleries, and a vibrant community.

- **Audubon Park:** This neighborhood is a nature-lovers paradise, offering green spaces and a local farmer's market. It's perfect for those who appreciate sustainability and a close-knit community.

- **Ivanhoe Village:** With a focus on arts and culture, this area is home to numerous galleries and boutiques. Don't miss its charming streets lined with historic buildings.

- **College Park:** Located northwest of Downtown, the neighborhood boasts beautiful lakes and streets lined with oak trees. It's a great place for a leisurely walk or a visit to one of the local restaurants.

Orlando's neighborhoods showcase its diverse culture, from the bustling energy of the downtown district to the tranquility of its hidden green spaces. Each area has a distinct character and offers a different experience, making Orlando a city where every street has its own story to tell.

Whatever neighborhood you find yourself in, you'll surely enjoy Orlando's year-round temperate climate as you check out the exciting events that shape its cultural landscape. Though Central Florida has a hot and humid climate, it's worth taking a closer look at the meteorological nuances to make sure your parade doesn't get rained on.

Orlando's Year-Round Climate and Events

Orlando is blessed with a climate that invites visitors year-round, making it a destination that's great for vacations all year round. Let's start by taking a closer look at what to expect in terms of weather, and then we'll have a look at some of the vibrant annual events that help define Orlando's character.

Weather Across the Seasons

Orlando's weather boasts pleasant temperatures and abundant sunshine, making it an ideal destination no matter when you visit. Here's a brief overview of what to expect each season:

- **spring:** Spring in Orlando brings warm and sunny days with temperatures ranging from the mid-60s to the high 80s °F (around 15 to 31 °C). It's a perfect time for outdoor activities, from exploring the city's gardens to enjoying festivals.

- **summer:** Summers are characterized by hot and humid weather with temperatures ranging from the high 80s to low 90s °F (around 31 to 34 °C). Frequent afternoon rain showers are common, providing relief from the heat. It's a great time to take advantage of Orlando's many indoor attractions and water parks.

- **fall:** Fall offers pleasant and less humid weather, with temperatures in the mid-70s to mid-80s °F (around 24 to 29 °C). It's a fantastic time to explore Orlando's parks and gardens and enjoy outdoor dining.

- **winter:** Winters in Orlando are mild, with temperatures ranging from the low 50s to mid-70s °F (around 10 to

24 °C). It's the perfect season to explore the city without the intense heat, making it a favorite for visitors.

Festivals and Events

As we've already made clear, Orlando isn't just about theme parks—it's also a city of numerous in-park and out-of-park festivities and celebrations that place Orlando on a global level with international cities across the world. Here are some of the unique annual festivals that give Orlando its distinctive character:

- **Epcot International Food and Wine Festival:** Hosted at Walt Disney World Resort, this festival runs from late summer into fall. It's a culinary journey featuring global cuisines, wines, and live entertainment.

- **Mardi Gras at Universal Orlando Resort:** Running from February through April, this celebration brings the spirit of New Orleans to Orlando with parades, concerts, and Cajun food.

- **Orlando Fringe Festival:** In May, this unjuried, uncensored performing arts festival presents a diverse range of shows, from theater to music and dance.

- **Florida Film Festival:** Held in April, this event showcases independent and international films, attracting filmmakers and cinephiles from around the world.

Other Special Events

Orlando's event calendar is packed with annual sporting events, concerts, and cultural happenings. Some notable mentions include:

- **Florida Cup:** This international soccer tournament takes place in January, attracting top teams from around the world.

- **Electric Daisy Carnival (EDC):** A massive electronic dance music festival held in November, EDC Orlando draws music enthusiasts for a weekend of non-stop beats and performances.

- **Orlando Shakespeare Theater:** Offering a variety of classic and contemporary plays, the theater provides a cultural experience throughout the year.

- **Orlando Magic Games:** If you're a basketball fan, catch an Orlando Magic game at the Amway Center during the NBA season.

- **EPCOT's Candlelight Processional:** Held in December, this is a moving reenactment of the Nativity story with a celebrity narrator and an orchestra.

Orlando is a city that never sleeps when it comes to events. No matter when you visit, there's always something exciting happening in this vibrant city.

As we've explored Orlando's neighborhoods, its climate, and its events, it's already becoming clear that this city offers much more than meets the eye. In subsequent chapters, we'll be continuing our exploration as we take a closer look at the diverse culinary scene, iconic out-of-park attractions, and the myriad of activities that make Orlando a true traveler's paradise, so don't stop flipping those pages!

Did You Know?

Orlando is home to a picturesque lake that holds a remarkable secret. Lake Eola, nestled in the heart of downtown Orlando, may appear to be just another inviting body of water, but it's in fact, a geological wonder with a fascinating history.

On the surface, it appears to be just any old lake, serving as a popular destination for both locals and tourists. Its lush greenery, swan boats, and iconic fountain create a postcard-perfect scene. But beneath its tranquil surface lies its ancient secret. Lake Eola's origins can be traced back to the formation of a sinkhole, a natural depression in the Earth's surface.

Sinkholes, formed by the dissolution of soluble bedrock, are not uncommon in Florida due to their unique geology, where much of the ground is actually hollow and filled with underground waterways. Lake Eola's sinkhole was created over thousands of years as water slowly eroded the limestone bedrock, causing the ground above to collapse, forming the basin we now know as the lake.

The lake reaches a staggering 80 feet at its lowest point, making it one of the deepest sinkhole lakes in the entire state!

Share Your Insights!

We're only one chapter deep so far, but you've already begun to uncover Orlando's hidden treasures, vibrant neighborhoods, and year-round charm. Now, it's your turn to become part of this ever-evolving story.

We're eager to hear about your adventures, insights, and personal discoveries as you explore Orlando, the city that truly has it all. Whether you're a first-time visitor or an Orlando enthusiast, your unique experiences and perspectives are invaluable.

Join us in creating a community of Orlando explorers by sharing your tips, stories, and photos. It's as simple as using the dedicated social media hashtag we've set up for this book: #DiscoverOrlandoGuide.

Here's how you can get involved:

- **share your tips:** Found a hidden gem in Orlando that's not in the book? Have some insider knowledge to add? Share your travel tips and recommendations using the hashtag. Your insights may help fellow travelers make the most of their Orlando experience and even be included in one of our future guidebooks!

- **post your photos:** Capture the essence of Orlando through your lens. Share your favorite snapshots of the city's landscapes, neighborhoods, and attractions. Tag them with #DiscoverOrlandoGuide so others can appreciate your view.

- **tell your story:** We all have our own unique Orlando story. Whether it's a heartwarming family adventure or a solo exploration that transformed your perspective, we want to hear it. Share your Orlando tales, and let your fellow readers be a part of your journey.

- **connect with fellow travelers:** Search for the #DiscoverOrlandoGuide hashtag to connect with like-minded travelers. Discover new perspectives, gather more travel ideas, and maybe even make new friends along the way.

By actively participating in our community, you're contributing to the ever-evolving story of Orlando. Your insights, recommendations, and experiences will enrich the collective knowledge of fellow explorers and help shape the future editions of this guide.

So, let's make Orlando's story a shared one. Join the conversation and be a part of the #DiscoverOrlandoGuide community. Your Orlando adventure has just begun, and there's so much more to discover ahead.

Time to Get Packing!

The chapters ahead are the keys to unlocking the full potential of your Orlando adventure. In them, we'll take a closer look at every aspect of planning your visit, from finding the ideal neighborhood to suit your style to discovering the best restaurants for family dining or a romantic evening out.

Whether you're looking for a cultural escapade, a family-friendly journey, or a solo backpacker's exploration, Orlando offers a diverse range of experiences to cater to every traveler's desires. We'll guide you through it all, step by step.

So, stay with us as the magic of this city is ready to unfold before your eyes, and you're just on the brink of crafting your own Orlando story. Now that we've painted a broad picture of Orlando let's get down to the nitty-gritty: Planning your own trip to this multifaceted city! Time to lug those old suitcases out of the closet and get going!

Chapter 2:

Planning Your Trip

Did you know that Orlando welcomed over 70 million visitors in 2022, ranking as the number one U.S. travel destination? (Media Image, 2023). The fact is, it's more than just a city—it's a place of enchantment and adventure, and not just in the Magic Kingdom. But with so much to see and do, how do you make the most of your Orlando adventure when you have a finite amount of time and want to see it all? That's where this chapter comes in.

When traveling to Orlando, it's important to plan wisely, ensuring that your vacation is a seamless and highly memorable experience. In this chapter, I'll be giving you some tricks and tips you can use to craft a well-rounded, smartly planned trip, taking into account seasonal timing, transportation, accommodations, and your personal travel budget. Whether you're a first-time traveler or a seasoned world explorer, the insights I'm going to give you on the ins and outs of Orlando will help you make the most of your Central Florida adventure.

Are you ready to start unlocking the magic of Orlando? Let's get started.

When to Visit

Choosing the right time to visit Orlando is your first step in putting together a memorable trip. Whether you prefer the thrill of peak season or the tranquility (and reduced crowds and lines) of off-peak times, Orlando caters to a variety of preferences all throughout the year.

Peak Season Versus Off-Peak Season

Peak season in Orlando typically falls during the summer months, from June to August, and the holiday season from mid-December to early January. During these times, the city experiences a surge in visitors, making it an exciting but jam-packed experience. Expect longer lines at attractions, including off-park attractions such as museums. The lines can be especially challenging at the theme parks during these times, and you can expect to pay significantly higher prices for accommodations.

On the flip side, the off-peak season, which spans from September to mid-December and January to May, can often allow for a more relaxed and budget-friendly experience. You'll find shorter lines, lower hotel rates, and milder weather. If I forgot to mention it before, we're well-known down here in Florida for the oppressive combination of heat and humidity. While we Floridians are used to it, visiting here in the summer can be a shock to the system for anyone from a cooler, more moderate climate.

The only downside of visiting Orlando during off-peak season is that some attractions or events may have reduced hours or be closed for maintenance.

Weather Tips

Orlando's climate is generally warm and humid. Here's a quick breakdown of what to expect each season:

- **spring (March to May):** Mild temperatures and low humidity make this an excellent time to visit and do a wide range of outdoor activities. Pack lightweight clothing and comfortable shoes.

- **summer (June to August):** As I already mentioned, the heat and humidity in Central Florida peak in the summer, so make sure to pack lightweight clothing, High-SPF waterproof sunscreen, and a refillable water bottle or flask to stay hydrated.

- **fall (September to November):** This season brings pleasant, mild weather. Pack layers, such as sweatshirts and sweaters, for cooler evenings.

- **winter (December to February):** It's the most comfortable season with mild temperatures. Bring a lightly insulated jacket, or layer with a windbreaker shell for cooler evenings.

Pro Tip: A tried and true method for enjoying attractions and rides at theme parks without all the waiting is to go while it's raining. Just make sure to pack lightweight plastic rain ponchos, and you'll stay dry while enjoying reduced waiting times.

Special Events Calendar

If you're interested in planning your trip around special events, Orlando has a vibrant calendar:

- **January: The EPCOT International Festival of the Arts** is an annual festival that began in 2017, showcasing visual, culinary, and performing arts. It lasts over a month, so if you're planning your trip at the beginning of the year, it's something you'll definitely want to check out.

- **February:** Universal Orlando's Mardi Gras celebration offers a taste of the Big Easy right in Central Florida. You'll feel just like you're carousing down Bourbon St. without actually having to plan a Louisiana stopover. The event features a parade and live performances.

- **March: EPCOT International Flower & Garden Festival** features stunning topiaries and gardens. If you've ever wondered how Edward Scissorhands got his start expertly sculpting hedges, it was right here. I'm just joshing you now, but for all you green-thumb havers out there: This event could be for you, and it runs all the way through the beginning of July, too!

- **April: SeaWorld Seven Seas Festival.** If you're one of those people who gets hungry when you visit the aquarium, this weekend's seafood fest might be for you. Don't worry, because at this shebang, Shamu's not going to be appearing on the menu—rather, he'll be arcing in the air above you as you slam down some delectable treats representing the best of culinary traditions from all around the world.

- **May:** The Orlando International Fringe Theatre Festival brings solo acts and theater troupes from all across the world for 14 days of fun. Running strong for over 30 years now, you never know what kind of interesting shows you'll catch at this un-juried open festival of the performing arts. Whether you're a theater aficionado or just looking for a unique cultural experience, the Fringe Festival has something for everyone.

- **June:** Enjoy Summer Spectacular nights at SeaWorld. Featuring light shows, DJs, and a breathtaking fireworks display, the Orlando park's night-time

23

festivities run all summer long, from late May to early September.

- **July:** Experience Independence Day celebrations with fireworks above both the Magic Kingdom and EPCOT. You can look forward to breathtaking views as we celebrate America Florida-style. You can look forward to music, live entertainment, and light shows, too.

- **August:** This month can certainly get steamy, and any kind of indoor activity is great to beat the heat. At the EPCOT International Food & Wine Festival, which runs from July through November, you can look forward to enjoying flavors from a diverse array of culinary traditions. Highlights include the bustling international marketplace, scavenger hunts, and a line of exclusive merchandise. The festival also features live music, giving you a chance to dance off all those calories.

- **September:** Magical Dining Month offers special dining deals run through the month. This annual festival allows residents and visitors alike to test the best the city has to offer. Running for six weeks starting in August, this popular program invites you to experience the wonders of Orlando's dining scene with three-course, *prix-fixe* dinners at many of our best restaurants,

- **October:** Halloween events at theme parks provide spooky fun. All the parks host special events for the entire family. Universal Studios transforms into a haunted haven with Halloween Horror Nights, featuring terrifying mazes, scare zones, and spine-tingling shows. Meanwhile, over at Disney, Mickey's Not-So-Scary Halloween Party at the Magic Kingdom offers a more family-friendly but still enchanting experience with Halloween parades and fireworks, not to mention trick-or-treating throughout the park. It's an ideal time to enjoy some chills and thrills during your visit to Orlando.

- **November:** If you're lucky enough to arrive the first week of the month, you'll be able to witness the transformation from October's spooky motifs to a captivating holiday theme. Both the Magic Kingdom and EPCOT host special events and decorations, transforming the parks into winter wonderlands. You can enjoy festive parades, dazzling light displays, and the enchanting Candlelight Processional featuring a celebrity narrator. It's the perfect way to get into the holiday spirit and create magical memories with your loved ones.

- **December:** The holiday spirit continues throughout December in Orlando. Many theme parks and attractions go all out with festive decorations and events. Universal Orlando's holiday celebrations are particularly noteworthy, featuring the Grinchmas Wholiday Spectacular and the Macy's Holiday Parade. Don't miss the chance to experience a warm Floridian Christmas with a touch of winter magic.

With this guide, you can choose the season that aligns best with your preferences and enjoy all that Orlando has to offer, tailored to your desired experience.

Transportation Around Orlando

Orlando has numerous transportation options that each help you make the most of your visit. In this section, we'll explore the various ways to get around Orlando, from shuttles to rideshares to the famous Wald Disney World Monorail System, and even unique options like renting a car, scooters, and bikes.

Public Transportation

Orlando offers tourists and residents alike a wide range of public transportation options that can help you navigate the city and reach further-flung destinations with ease. Lynx, the Central Florida Regional Transportation Authority, operates a network of buses that connect various parts of the city, making it an affordable way to move around. The Lynx bus system is particularly useful for getting to places not directly accessible by tourist shuttles or other modes of transportation.

Rideshare Apps (Uber and Lyft)

If you're looking for convenience and flexibility, ridesharing services like Uber and Lyft are readily available in Orlando. These options are especially convenient for trips to and from the airport or for reaching attractions not well-served by public transportation.

Car Rentals

Renting a car in Orlando provides the freedom to explore the city and its surrounding areas at your own pace. While the city's public transportation is improving, having a car can be a valuable asset, especially if you plan on visiting destinations beyond Orlando's main tourist areas. Pros of renting a car include the ability to go off the beaten path, visit less crowded attractions, and make day trips to nearby cities like Tampa or Miami. Several car rental companies operate at the airport and throughout the city, making it easy to find a vehicle that suits your needs. However, it's essential to consider parking fees, which can add up, especially at popular tourist destinations.

Fun Transportation Options

Orlando also offers unique and fun ways to explore the city. Scooter and bike rentals have become increasingly popular, especially in the downtown area. You can use various apps to rent electric scooters or bicycles for short trips or sightseeing adventures. These options are eco-friendly and provide a different perspective on the city, allowing you to enjoy the open air and pleasant weather while getting around.

Walt Disney World Monorail System

If you're planning on exploring the magic of Walt Disney World Resort, the Monorail System is an iconic and efficient mode of transportation. Disney's Monorail is a unique way to travel within the resort, connecting select hotels and the Magic Kingdom and EPCOT theme parks. This elevated train system is not only practical but also offers a touch of Disney charm to your journey.

The Monorail System is made up of three separate lines:

- **resort monorail:** This line serves three Disney resorts—Disney's Grand Floridian Resort & Spa, Disney's Polynesian Village Resort, and Disney's Contemporary Resort. It's a convenient way to access the Magic Kingdom and the transportation and ticket center.

- **express monorail:** This line connects the Transportation and Ticket Center (TTC) with the Magic Kingdom. It's a direct route from the TTC to the park, making it a quick and hassle-free way to reach the Magic Kingdom's entrance.

- **EPCOT monorail:** If you plan to visit EPCOT, this monorail line will take you there. The route provides scenic views of the resort and the park, enhancing your overall Disney experience.

The Monorail System not only gets you to your destination but also provides beautiful views of the resort, especially during the evening. It's a fun and engaging way to travel, especially for families with young children who tend to be enthralled by the whole experience.

Where to Stay

When planning your trip to Orlando, one of the key decisions you'll need to make is where to stay. The city offers a wide range of accommodation options to suit different budgets and travel preferences. Whether you're looking for luxury or affordability, Orlando has something to offer to every type of traveler.

Types of Accommodations

Luxury

For travelers seeking a lavish and pampered experience, Orlando boasts a variety of luxury accommodations. These high-end options include upscale hotels and resorts, often with extravagant amenities and services. Luxury accommodations are ideal for couples celebrating a special occasion or families looking to splurge.

Affordable

If you're looking to maximize your budget while still enjoying a comfortable stay, Orlando offers plenty of affordable options. These include budget-friendly hotels, motels, and vacation rentals, providing value for money and convenience. Affordable accommodations are a great choice for solo travelers and families seeking a practical and economical stay.

Different Options For All Kinds of Travelers

Families and Convenience-Seekers

Families visiting Orlando often find that staying in a hotel or resort with family-friendly amenities is the way to go. Many resorts offer spacious suites and activities tailored to kids, making it a memorable experience for the whole family. Some popular family-friendly options include Disney's Contemporary Resort, Universal's Cabana Bay Beach Resort, and the Hilton Orlando Bonnet Creek.

Budget-Minded Families, Penny-Saving Retirees, and Solo Travelers

For travelers who prioritize cost-effectiveness, Orlando offers numerous budget-friendly options, such as well-rated motels and vacation rentals. Tru by Hilton and the Monumental Movieland Hotel are both affordable choices for tourists on a budget.

Couples

Couples looking for a romantic escape can opt for intimate and luxurious hotels. Orlando's boutique and high-end accommodations provide the perfect setting for a romantic getaway. If you have the budget that affords a big splurge, consider shelling out for a stay at The Ritz-Carlton Orlando, Waldorf Astoria Orlando, or even the ultra-luxe Four Seasons Resort Orlando at Walt Disney World.

Examples of Different Price Ranges

Orlando Hotels can run the whole gamut, from budget-friendly to ultra-luxe. Let's take a look at the price ranges we're talking about for nightly room rates, both on-peak and off-peak season.

Luxury Price Range

At any of these highly refined options, you're bound to find numerous perks and creature comforts that'll make your experience unforgettable, though some of them might cost you an arm and a leg.

- **Four Seasons Resort Orlando at Walt Disney World:** A five-star resort with a water park, golf, and multiple dining options. A room at this place comes with some sticker shock, as it sets you back upwards of $2000 per night.

- **The Ritz-Carlton Orlando, Grande Lakes:** A luxurious lakeside retreat offering elegant rooms, a world-class spa, and fine dining. Prices typically range from $700 all the way up to $1200 per night if you're booking closer to your travel date.

- **Disney's Grand Floridian Resort & Spa:** For visitors heading to Walt Disney World, the Grand Floridian Resort offers lavish accommodations with prices starting at $480 or so per night.

- **Waldorf Astoria Orlando:** An upscale resort with a golf course, spa, and exquisite dining options. This is a more affordable version of luxury vs. the Four Seasons, Ritz-Carlton, and Grand Floridian, with room rates generally ranging from as low as $215 up to $790 per night during the more popular times to visit.

Affordable Price Range

- **Hard Rock Hotel at Universal Orlando:** Located next to Universal Orlando, this world-famous hotel chain offers a luxurious yet laid-back experience. Prices typically range from $250 to $450 per night.

- **Hyatt Regency Orlando:** Situated on International Drive, the Hyatt Regency Orlando provides an upscale and serene experience, with prices ranging from $200 to $400 per night.

- **Gaylord Palms:** If you're traveling with your family, the Gaylord Palms is a fantastic option. It offers a wide range of family-friendly amenities, and prices generally range from $150 to $400 per night.

- **The Park Plaza Hotel:** Located on the picturesque Park Avenue in Winter Park, this boutique hotel is ideal for a peaceful stay and offers rates starting from around $200 per night.

- **Grand Bohemian Hotel Orlando, Autograph Collection:** This stylish boutique hotel offers an upscale experience at a reasonable price, making it a great choice for travelers on a budget. Prices typically range from $150 to $300 per night.

- **The Wellborn:** Nestled near Thornton Park, The Wellborn is a modern boutique hotel with understated charm. Prices typically range from $150 to $250 per night.

- **The Delaney Hotel:** This contemporary hotel is great for business travelers and offers a comfortable stay at reasonable rates. Prices generally range from $100 to $200 per night.

- **EO Inn:** Situated in downtown Orlando, the EO Inn is an affordable boutique hotel perfect for those looking for laid-back local charm, but make sure to book well in advance as there are only 21 rooms. Prices usually start around $100 per night, going up to around $180.

- **Tru by Hilton:** For budget-conscious travelers, Tru by Hilton provides comfortable and affordable accommodations, with rates starting from around $70 to $120 per night.

By considering your travel style, budget, and the type of experience you desire, you can choose the perfect accommodation that suits your needs in Orlando. Whether you prefer the lap of luxury or are focused on stretching your vacation dollars, Orlando has a place for you to call home during your stay.

How Much Money to Budget For Your Trip

Let's face it: an Orlando really can break the bank if you don't plan it right, but it doesn't have to. Here are some general tips for saving money while still enjoying your trip:

- Consider traveling during the off-peak season to find better deals on accommodations and attractions.

- Look for combo tickets or passes that offer discounts on multiple attractions.

- Plan your meals and snacks to avoid overpriced dining options inside theme parks.

- Use public transportation or rideshares to save on car rental and parking fees.

- Check for discounts and deals on attractions' official websites or through third-party vendors.

- Explore the many free and low-cost attractions available, such as parks, museums, and outdoor activities.

Ticket Costs for Popular Attractions

Here's a breakdown of estimated ticket costs for some of Orlando's popular attractions:

- **Walt Disney World:** Ticket prices vary depending on the park, type of ticket, and time of year. On average, a single-day one-park ticket at the base price can range from $109 to $189 per adult, sales tax not included. Multi-day tickets offer some savings. Disney often offers discounts for military personnel and Florida residents.

- **Universal Orlando Resort:** A single-day park-to-park ticket, which allows you to traverse between Universal Studios and Islands of Adventure, starts at $119, but prices can go up during peak times. Multi-day tickets and park-to-park tickets provide better value.

- **SeaWorld Orlando:** A single-day ticket starts at around $85 for adults with advance purchase discounts applied.

- **Gatorland:** This budget-friendly attraction offers standard adult day passes for $32.99.

- **Kennedy Space Center Visitor Complex:** Admission costs roughly $75 for adults and $45 for kids. Discounts are often available for children, seniors, active-duty military members, and their family members. Look out for special prices throughout the year on regular adult admission, too.

- **ICON Park:** ICON Park itself is free to enter. However, if you plan to ride The Wheel, tickets are $29.99 per person.

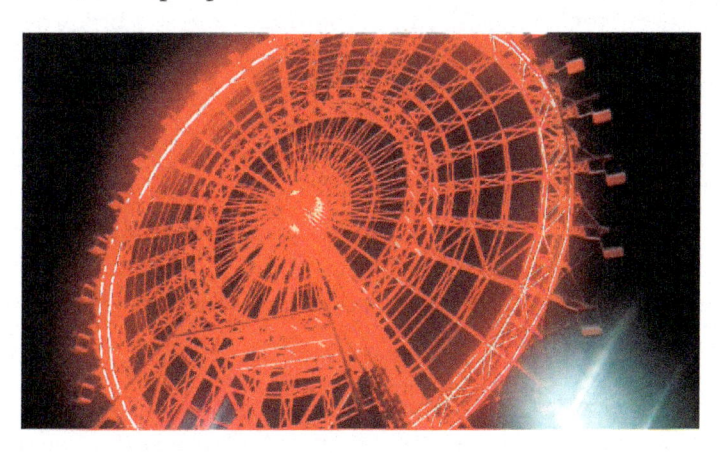

Did You Know?

Did you know that Disney's Monorail system, often seen as a symbol of futuristic transportation, was first introduced to the public at Disneyland in 1959? Walt Disney himself believed in the potential of monorails as efficient and stylish transportation, and he pioneered their use in the theme park setting. Over six decades later, the Disney Monorail remains a beloved and iconic part of the Walt Disney World experience.

The system boasts a fascinating history. It all began with the Mark I Monorail. In the early stages of Disneyland's development, Walt Disney envisioned a monorail system as part of Tomorrowland. However, it took until 1958 for two Imagineers to introduce him to the Alweg Corporation's monorail from Germany.

What set the Alweg design apart was its unique straddle-beam track, which seamlessly blended with the park's landscape. This design not only impressed Walt but also offered a near-silent operation, thanks to electric propulsion and rubber wheels, ensuring a distraction-free experience for guests.

Walt Disney's collaboration with Alweg led to the creation of the Disneyland Alweg Monorail System, which opened on June 14, 1959. It featured two trains with three cabins each, characterized by the now-iconic bubble top in front. Although Walt's vision extended to worldwide mass transportation, the initial purpose of the Disneyland Alweg Monorail System was purely entertainment.

It didn't serve as transportation for guests until 1961, marking the beginning of a new chapter in monorail history. So, the next time you embark on a monorail adventure at a Disney park, remember that it all started with the innovative Mark I Monorail, which introduced a touch of tomorrow to the world of today (Glover, 2013).

Share Your Insights!

As we conclude this chapter of your Orlando adventure, I once again invite you to share your insights, tips, and experiences with the community. Whether you've uncovered hidden cheap hotel rates in Orlando, have a unique perspective on ticket price hacks and how to get the best rates and packages, or simply want to share your magical moments, your input is valuable. Join the conversation by using the hashtag #DiscoverOrlandoGuide on social media to connect with fellow explorers and share your insights!

You're Almost There

You've meticulously crafted your plans, and your bags are nearly packed. The anticipation is building, and you're on the brink of embarking on an unforgettable journey filled with magic and wonder—the theme parks await! In the upcoming chapter, we'll jump right into exploring the heart of Orlando's enchanting world of entertainment.

Get ready to explore the thrills, enchantment, and endless adventures that the theme parks have in store for you. Can you almost feel the excitement and thrill? You're almost there, primed to step into a realm of imagination and excitement. So, let's go! It's time to dive into the enchanting realm of Orlando's theme parks together!

Chapter 3:

The Magic of Theme Parks

Theme parks are the lifeblood of Orlando, where every moment is an opportunity for enchantment and exhilaration. These captivating wonderlands offer a gateway to worlds of fantasy, adventure, and endless fun. In this chapter, we will be your guiding star through the thrilling universe of Orlando's major theme parks, providing you with a wealth of knowledge, insider secrets, and hidden gems to ensure your visits are nothing short of extraordinary. Get ready to take a fantastical trip in which we'll explore the ins and outs of Orlando's thrilling theme parks, where every twist and turn holds the promise of a new adventure.

Walt Disney World

Disney is often referred to as the happiest place on Earth, and it truly is a sprawling universe of magic, wonder, and enchantment. To fully embrace the magic that awaits, from the Magic Kingdom to the iconic EPCOT dome, it's essential to have some key information and tips within easy reach when it comes time to plan your Disney vacation.

Things to Know Before You Go

First, let's take a look at some of the basics: Walt Disney World is open year-round, with daily operating hours that can vary depending on the park and season. In terms of ticketing, Disney offers a wide variety of options, including single-day tickets, multi-day passes, and annual passes. Prices can fluctuate, so it's wise to check their website for current rates.

Must-Ride Attractions

Now, let's talk about the heart-pounding excitement that Walt Disney World has to offer. From the moment you step into the parks, you'll be greeted by iconic attractions that have become staples of the Disney experience. Must-ride attractions include

Space Mountain, where you'll embark o adventure through the cosmos. The Haunted spine-tingling journey through a ghostly estate don't miss the Pirates of the Caribbean, whe with swashbuckling buccaneers.

Meeting Your Favorite Disney Characters

Meeting beloved Disney characters is a dream come true for many visitors. At Walt Disney World, you'll have the opportunity to meet characters like Mickey Mouse, Elsa from Frozen, and so many more. Keep an eye out for character meet-and-greet locations throughout the parks, including the famous Chef Mickey's breakfast, and don't forget to have your camera ready for those unforgettable photo ops.

Secret Tips for Disney World

As you navigate the enchanting world of Disney, it's worth knowing a few secrets that can enhance your experience. To avoid long lines, consider using the Disney Genie+ system, which allows you to reserve access to select attractions in advance. Also, utilizing time-saving tools, such as the mobile food ordering app, can allow you to skip the lines at dining locations. For hidden treats, venture to Storybook Treats in Fantasyland for delectable ice cream concoctions, or head to Sleepy Hollow for to-die-for waffle sandwiches.

Universal Orlando

To make the most of your visit to this star-studded, chair-gripping, action-packed park, let's start with some essential information.

Things to Know Before You Go

Universal Orlando is open throughout the year, with operational hours subject to change. Be sure to check their official website for the latest information on park hours, ticket prices, and any special offers.

The Coolest Rides

Now, let's talk about the thrilling rides that await you at Universal Orlando. Aside from the epic Spiderman coaster, one of the standout attractions is the Incredible Hulk's equally thrilling ride. The gravity-defying coaster propels you through a high-speed, zero-gravity roll, making it a must-try for adrenaline junkies. The Hogwarts Express, a magical train journey, transports visitors between Universal Studios and Islands of Adventure, offering a unique and enchanting experience.

All Things Harry Potter

Aside from the Hogwarts Express, Universal is also home to the Wizarding World of Harry Potter. There, you can immerse yourself in the magic of J.K. Rowling's universe as you explore Hogwarts Castle, sip butterbeer at the Three Broomsticks, and shop for wands at Ollivanders. Don't forget to experience the incredible rides, including Harry Potter and the Forbidden Journey and Escape from Gringotts.

Universal's Hidden Secrets

Universal Orlando holds many hidden gems and secrets waiting to be discovered. Keep an eye out for Easter eggs and references to your favorite movies and characters throughout the park. For less-crowded spots to snap great photos, head to areas like the picturesque Port of Entry in Islands of Adventure or the New York area.

Other Theme Parks and Attractions

Orlando isn't just about the big theme parks—it's a dynamic city that offers a wide variety of exciting attractions and experiences that go way beyond the most popular tourist destinations. Let's explore some of these unique sites and attractions that also promise visitors a ton of fun.

SeaWorld Orlando and Aquatica Park

SeaWorld Orlando offers a delightful blend of marine life shows and thrilling rides, making it a must-visit destination in Orlando. The park is renowned for its captivating marine life shows, where you can witness the incredible intelligence and agility of dolphins, whales, and other exciting sea creatures. These shows, led by charismatic trainers, can be both educational and entertaining.

One of the highlights at SeaWorld is the opportunity to get up close and personal with these animals. You'll have the opportunity to touch and feed dolphins and even swim with them for a unique and unforgettable experience.

For those seeking an adrenaline rush, SeaWorld also features a number of exciting rides. Mako, Kraken, and Manta are some of the most popular coasters in the park. SeaWorld also plays an essential role in marine conservation. During your visit, you can learn about the park's conservation efforts and how they're working to protect marine life.

The park offers a wide variety of dining options, from casual to fine dining, making it easy for you to stay all day! With its unique mix of aquatic wonders and thrilling rides, SeaWorld provides a truly unforgettable experience for the whole family.

Aquatica Park, part of the SeaWorld complex, is your go-to destination if you're seeking a refreshing escape from the Orlando heat. This water park offers a variety of attractions to keep you cool. And the best part is that your SeaWorld ticket gets you access to both parks!

Visitors hop next door to Aquatica to experience its thrilling waterslides and rides. From heart-pounding drops to more relaxed, family-friendly options, there's something for everyone. The giant wave pools at Aquatica offer the soothing and exhilarating experience of riding the waves. It's a great place to swim and relax in a beautiful setting.

For a leisurely adventure, hop on one of the park's lazy rivers. You'll float along at your own pace, taking in the picturesque surroundings. Whether you're an adrenaline junkie or prefer a more relaxed day on the lazy creek, this park has something for everyone.

LEGOLAND Florida Resort

For families with young kids, LEGOLAND Florida Resort is a dream come true. This park is tailored for a fun and interactive experience that kids of all ages will enjoy, boasting an array of rides and attractions designed with younger children in mind. From the Duplo Valley to the LEGO Kingdoms, there's a world of adventure to explore.

The park is brimming with intricate LEGO creations, making it an excellent place to unleash your creativity and imagination. The attention to detail is astounding, and you'll find incredible LEGO sculptures throughout the park.

LEGOLAND offers a number of different shows and entertainment, providing a well-rounded experience for the whole family. The LEGO Movie World is a particularly beloved section of the park. You'll find various dining options inside the park, including healthy choices for kids and adults alike, making it easy to stay for a full day of adventure.

With its focus on family fun and creativity, LEGOLAND Florida Resort offers a different kind of fun that incorporates learning and play.

Gatorland

If you're in search of a truly unique and thrilling experience in Orlando, Gatorland should be at the top of your list. Often referred to as the "Alligator Capital of the World," this wildlife park offers an up-close and personal encounter with these incredible reptiles.

Gatorland isn't your typical theme park—it's a place where you can observe live alligators and crocodiles in their natural habitat. Imagine holding a live gator, taking memorable photos with these fascinating creatures, and learning about them from experienced handlers. The Gator Encounters at this park provide a truly unique opportunity for curious visitors.

For the adrenaline junkies, Gatorland offers the Screamin' Gator Zip Line adventure. You'll zip line over alligator breeding marshes, creating an unforgettable, heart-pounding experience. But the excitement doesn't end there. Gatorland is world-renowned for the up-close encounters with various animals it offers, including parrots, tortoises, and, of course, gators! The park's friendly staff is always ready to educate and entertain visitors, making every interaction memorable.

Gatorland also hosts shows and demonstrations featuring expert trainers and the park's star alligators, showcasing their impressive strength and natural behaviors. These shows are both educational and entertaining, offering a deeper appreciation for these incredible creatures.

For a more leisurely experience, take a stroll along Gatorland's Boardwalk. You'll be surrounded by the beauty of nature as you observe hundreds of gators in their natural Everglades environment.

Fun Spot America

Fun Spot America offers classic theme park fun without the massive crowds. Located in Orlando, this park is a fantastic addition to your itinerary. Offering visitors a variety of thrilling rides, including roller coasters and go-karts. If you're a thrill-seeker—you simply can't miss old-timey thrills like the famous White Lightning wooden coaster.

The park prides itself on its family-friendly atmosphere, making it the perfect destination for visitors of all ages. Whether you're traveling with family, friends, or both, everyone is sure to have a blast. One of the standout features of Fun Spot America is its affordability compared to the big parks. You'll find reasonably priced tickets and a range of deals and packages, ensuring that you get great value for your money.

Beyond the rides, you can also look forward to enjoying some classic arcade games, and, if you're lucky, even live entertainment shows during your visit. It's an ideal place to create lasting memories with loved ones. With two convenient locations in Orlando, you have options to choose from, making it easy to fit Fun Spot America into your Orlando adventure.

Did You Know?

Amid the sights and thrills of Orlando's world-famous theme parks lies a natural wonder that often goes unnoticed. The Orlando Wetlands, located in east Orange County, is a hidden gem that beckons those seeking a different kind of adventure. What sets this place apart is its role as a sanctuary for wildlife, particularly those that find themselves on the Florida Wildlife Conservation Commission's Threatened and Endangered Wildlife list.

This vast wetland area provides refuge to over 30 species of wildlife facing the challenges of conservation (*40 Fun Orlando Facts*, 2014). From majestic wading birds to the mesmerizing reptiles that call it home, the Orlando Wetlands offers a rare opportunity to witness nature's resilience.

Exploring this unique ecosystem not only offers a peaceful escape from the hustle and bustle of the city but also grants a firsthand look at the delicate balance of life in a region that often takes the spotlight for its thrilling attractions. The Orlando Wetlands is a great example of the rich biodiversity that Florida boasts, and it's a must-visit for anyone looking to connect with the natural world while on vacation.

Share Your Insights!

The deeper we go into exploring Orlando and uncovering its hidden gems, the more we want to hear from you, the intrepid and savvy explorers whose stories we depend on! Do you have your own favorite tips for navigating the theme parks? Perhaps you've uncovered a secret spot in Universal Orlando that's perfect for capturing stunning photos. Or maybe you've even had an unforgettable close call with the incredible wildlife at Gatorland yourself, Steve Irwin-style.

Share your insights and experiences with us! We invite you to join the conversation and become a part of our vibrant community of Orlando enthusiasts. Connect with fellow travelers, share your discoveries, and exchange valuable tips and recommendations.

Use the hashtag #DiscoverOrlandoGuide on your social media platforms to let us in on your adventures and to connect with like-minded explorers. Your insights could make someone else's Orlando experience even more magical. So, go ahead, share your Orlando story, and let's make the most of this incredible journey together!

Once You've Had Your Fill of Action, How About a Change of Pace?

After all the rollercoasters, and once you've had your fill of fairy-tale magic, it's time to step into a different part of Orlando—a world where nature reigns supreme. Amidst the thrilling theme parks and vibrant attractions, there's a veritable oasis of tranquility just waiting to be discovered.

You might not know it, but Orlando offers a remarkable variety of natural wonders and outdoor adventures, making it the perfect destination for those who seek a change of pace from the bustling excitement of the city and all the theme parks.

In the next chapter, we'll take you on a virtual tour of some of the breathtaking natural landscapes that Orlando and Central

Florida have to offer. From lush gardens to serene lakes, from wildlife encounters to scenic hiking trails, you'll find that an Orlando vacation doesn't have to just be about the popular attractions—it can also be considered as a travel destination where you have ample opportunity to take in the beauty of the great outdoors. So, get ready to explore the more serene side of Orlando, where nature takes center stage.

Chapter 4:

Nature Time in Orlando

Though its world is known for its towering rides and enchanting theme parks, Orlando is also a gateway to a world of natural wonders. In this chapter, we invite you to step away from the excitement of roller coasters and the long lines that so often accompany them to explore the diverse and stunning natural beauty that surrounds the Orlando area, including all of Central Florida, as well as both coasts.

You see, Florida is a rather narrow peninsula that is quite easy to get around; even sunny Miami's not too far if you have a car and the will to get there. So, if you're headed to Orlando and want to add some beach trips, or even jet skiing or deep sea fishing, to your itinerary, know that you're not just limited to testing your luck at bird watching in swamps full of chomping gators.

Right inside Orlando itself, beyond the theme parks' dazzling attractions and endless family-friendly entertainment, there's a rich array of tranquil, natural landscapes that await your discovery. From lush wetlands and crystal-clear springs to sprawling parks and serene nature spots—if you've ever wondered what secrets lie hidden in the shadow of Orlando's iconic attractions, prepare to find out.

It's time to swap your mouse ears for a pair of binoculars, the rails of roller coaster rides for scenic nature paths, and your theme park thrills for tranquil kayak trips. It's time to dive straight into the heart of the natural world of Orlando and its environs.

Parks and Nature Spots

When you think of Florida's natural wonders, the Everglades are bound to be at the top of the list. This unique and expansive ecosystem is a must-visit for nature lovers seeking a glimpse into the heart of wild Florida. Here, we delve into the secrets of the Everglades and the reasons why it's a vital stop on your nature adventure.

The Everglades: A Natural Marvel

Nestled just a few hours south of Orlando, the Everglades National Park is a UNESCO World Heritage Site and International Biosphere Reserve. Known as the "River of Grass," it's the largest tropical wilderness of any kind in any eastern U.S. state. The Everglades are unlike any other place in the world, featuring a mosaic of habitats, including sawgrass prairies, cypress swamps, and mangrove forests.

Reasons to Visit Everglades National Park on Your Orlando Adventure

The Everglades offer an unparalleled opportunity to connect with nature. Here are some reasons why it's a must-visit:

- **Wildlife spotting.** The Everglades are home to an astonishing array of wildlife, including alligators, manatees, a variety of bird species, and the elusive Florida panther.

- **See a unique ecosystem.** It's one of the most unique and fragile ecosystems in the world, with a mix of freshwater and saltwater habitats.

- **Take an airboat adventure.** Take an exhilarating airboat ride through the sawgrass prairies for a chance to spot wildlife and experience the iconic Everglades.

- **Learn a thing or two.** The park offers numerous visitor centers and ranger-led programs, providing insight into the park's ecology, wildlife, and conservation efforts.

Wekiwa Springs: A Local Gem

The Everglades are just the beginning of exploring Florida's natural treasures. The refreshing waters of Wekiwa Springs lure visitors, too. Just a short drive from Orlando, Wekiwa Springs State Park offers a refreshing escape into nature. This local favorite is a sanctuary of crystal-clear waters, lush forests, and abundant wildlife. Here, visitors can immerse themselves in a variety of outdoor activities, making it a perfect spot for a day of relaxation, natural adventure, and fun.

Activities at Wekiwa Springs

- **swimming:** Wekiwa Springs is, of course, famous for its natural spring, which maintains a comfortable 72-degree temperature year-round. You can take a dip in the spring and enjoy the crystal-clear waters, surrounded by the scenic beauty of the park.

- **canoeing and kayaking:** Explore the pristine Wekiva River that flows through the park. You can rent canoes and kayaks from the park concessionaire or bring your own. Paddle down the river and observe the diverse plant and animal life that thrives in this environment.

- **hiking and biking:** The park features several miles of hiking and biking trails, providing opportunities to venture deeper into the wilderness. Keep an eye out for native flora and fauna along the way.

- **picnicking and camping:** There are also picnic areas with grills, making it an excellent place for a family outing. If you want to extend your stay, the park has a campground with both dispersed "primitive" camping and full-facility campsites available for both tents and RVs.

- **wildlife watching:** Birdwatching and wildlife viewing are popular activities in the park. The diverse ecosystems at the Springs support a wide range of species, from songbirds to turtles and deer.

Other Nature Parks and Areas Near Orlando

Apart from Wekiwa Springs, Orlando boasts several other natural parks and preserves, each offering its unique charm:

- **Biscayne National Park:** Located a few hours south of Miami, this national park is famous for its underwater coral reefs and marine life. Snorkeling and scuba diving enthusiasts will find this place to be a haven for aquatic exploration.

- **Timucuan Ecological & Historical Preserve:** Just a short drive from Orlando, this preserve covers thousands of acres of unspoiled wetlands and historical sites, providing a glimpse into Florida's natural and cultural history.

- **Shingle Creek:** Known as the "Headwaters to the Everglades," Shingle Creek is a serene waterway in Orlando. Visitors can enjoy paddling, fishing, and bird-watching along its banks.

- **Moss Park and Split Oak Forest Park:** These parks offer a range of activities, from hiking and biking to fishing and bird-watching. Moss Park features a picturesque lake, while Split Oak Forest Park is known for its wildlife and nature trails.

Bird-Watching in Orlando

You might not know it, but Orlando is a bird-watchers paradise, with numerous locations where you can observe a wide variety of avian species. Popular bird-watching spots include:

- **Orlando Wetlands Park:** A unique birding destination, this park provides opportunities to spot various bird species. It's a designated site on the Great Florida Birding Trail.

- **Disney Wilderness Preserve:** This pristine preserve near Orlando is home to a diverse bird population, including waterfowl, wading birds, and raptors.

- **Gatorland:** Besides its reptilian inhabitants, Gatorland, which we already highlighted in the previous chapter, is a prime location for bird-watching. You can spot numerous species here, including herons and egrets.

- **Lake Apopka Wildlife Drive:** This scenic drive offers excellent bird-watching opportunities. Keep an eye out for bald eagles, red-shouldered hawks, and various waterfowl.

- **Orlando Wetlands Park:** As mentioned earlier, this park is a top destination for bird enthusiasts. You can spot everything from sandhill cranes to warblers in its diverse wetland habitats.

With all these natural wonders awaiting you in Orlando, I hope it's whet your proverbial bird whistle, and you're ready for more nature action. In the next section, I'll cue you in on a number of exciting nature tours, boat rides, and opportunities to encounter local wildlife in and around Orlando.

Fun Nature Tours

Boat Tours Near Orlando

One of the most peaceful and scenic ways to experience Orlando's natural beauty is through a boat tour. Whether you prefer a leisurely cruise or a thrilling high-speed airboat or motorboat ride, these boat tours offer a unique perspective on the region's lush landscapes and wildlife. Here's just a glimpse of the wide range of tour options available:

Orlando Lake Tours in Windermere

This trusted local operator offers a variety of tours in the Butler chain of lakes on a 25-foot pontoon boat that fits up to 10 passengers, including options for both shared cruises and exclusive chartered private tours. Depending on the day and where exactly you'll be cruising, you can look forward to up-close encounters with Florida's wildlife, all while enjoying the scenic beauty of Orlando's lakes.

Current rates are just $25 per person for a 75-minute tour. For more details, check out their website: www.orlandolaketours.com or call (407) 883-0110.

Spirit of the Swamp in Kissimmee

If the exciting thrills of a high-speed airboat are more your style, you might want to check out Spirit of the Swamp. Guests can look forward to seeing a wide array of natural beauty, including swamp-dwelling creatures of all types. Heck, you might even spot a gator or two if you're lucky. Step aboard this luxury airboat tour, and you're in for a real treat.

Current rates for adults are $55 for an hour and $50 for kids. To extend your ride to a full 90 minutes of fun, that'll set you back an additional 15 bucks on each ticket for grown-ups and kids alike. For more information, have a peek at their website, spiritoftheswamp.com, or give them a call at (321) 689-6893

Boggy Creek Airboat Adventures in Kissimmee

If you're looking to book an airboat ride and want to go with a tour operator that offers a wide variety of options, Boggy Creek is your best bet for swamp-based fun in the Orlando area. Not only do they offer standard day rides and adventure tour packages, but they also have sunset cruises and thrilling night rides, too! Alligators are known to be nocturnal predators, and while you can spot them by day from time to time, it's best to try to spot them during their prime hunting hours. What could be more thrilling than spotting a live gator snatch up its prey illuminated by the glow of a flashlight on a nighttime swamp tour?

If this sounds like something up your alley, check out Boggy Creek's website: https://bcairboats.com/ or give them a call at

(407) 344-9550. Rates vary depending on the package you're interested in, but they're all quite reasonably priced. There's even a Supreme Package available that includes lunch, access to a gem mine tour, a butterfly feeding zone garden, and a commemorative cup to take home with you.

Kayaking Near Orlando

For a more hands-on and tranquil nature waterborne experience, consider kayaking. Orlando offers numerous waterways and picturesque locations to practice this fun and near-zero learning curb sport. Whether you're a beginner or an experienced kayaker, there's a spot for everyone!

King's Landing at Rocks Spring Run in Apopka

King's Landing in Apopka, right on the edge of Rocks Spring Run, is for kayaking enthusiasts. Picture yourself paddling down crystal-clear waters that wind through a landscape adorned with majestic oaks draped in Spanish moss. For just $69, you can have an entire afternoon of kayaking fun in a double kayak or opt for a single kayak at $49. If you're up for an adventure, consider renting a canoe instead of a kayak to save some bucks. It's a hidden gem, for sure.

For more information, check out their website here: kingslandingfl.com

The Paddling Center at Shingle Creek in Kissimmee

The Paddling Center in Kissimmee offers a convenient option for kayaking right near the busy heart of Orlando, conveniently off Highway 192. For a budget-friendly price of $45, you can rent a tandem kayak for two hours or go solo with a single kayak for $30. The paddling trails may be shorter, but the breathtaking views and stunning scenery, including live alligators, more than makeup for the fact that this centrally-located creek doesn't offer longer itineraries

For more information on booking your kayak adventure, visit their website: paddlingcenter.com.

St. Johns River Cruises at Blue Spring State Park

If you have a passion for manatees, Blue Spring State Park, just a 45-minute drive from Orlando, is your go-to destination. Located in Orange City, it's one of the prime spots to witness these majestic creatures in their natural habitat. And the best part is that you can rent kayaks from St. Johns River Cruises for up to four hours! For those less keen on the idea of kayaking, canoeing, or paddleboarding, all of which are available, there's also a guided boat cruise tour.

The admission fee to the state park is $6 per vehicle, and for more information about planning your kayak adventure, visit St. John River Cruises' website here: bluespringadventures.com/kayak-canoe-paddleboard-rentals (Alvin, 2023)

Animal Encounters

While kayaking through the natural beauty of Orlando is a fantastic way to connect with the environment, there are also incredible opportunities to get up close and personal with exotic wildlife species in the city without getting in the water. Orlando boasts a range of animal encounters that allow you to witness and interact with fascinating creatures from all over the world!

In this section, we'll take a look at some of the top options for land-loving exotic animal enthusiasts, making sure you can get all your critter-viewing in without even having to get your feet wet.

Safari Wilderness Ranch in Lakeland

Safari Wilderness Ranch offers both in-car safari tours and thrilling expeditions on camelback. This is a great place to get you up close and personal with a variety of animals. The ranch features a wide range of endangered species you may have never heard of before, including:

- **the mighty eland:** The largest of African antelopes; while they're not native to Florida, you'll recognize them by their distinctive spiral-horned appearance. These animals are typically found in the savannas and open grasslands of Africa.

- **the sly springbok:** Another species of antelope, Springbok is medium-sized and, like the eland, is native to Africa. They're well-known for their incredible jumping ability, often leaping into the air with impressive grace. You can easily spot them by looking out for their reddish-brown coat and striking white facial markings.

- **the majestic blackbuck antelope:** Blackbuck antelope are from the Indian subcontinent. They're characterized by their striking black-and-white coloration, with males typically having long, spiraled horns. Blackbucks are known for their speed and agility.

- **the amazing fallow deer:** Also not native to Florida but rather to Eurasia, this species of deer does, in fact, have established populations in various parts of the United States. You'll recognize them by their beautiful spotted coats, which can range from white to various shades of brown.

- **the graceful water buffalo:** Though also not native to Florida water buffalos are well-adapted to aquatic environments and are often found in wetlands and marshy areas in their native Asia. The species is known for its distinctive curved horns and robust build.

The safari offered at the ranch isn't just about entertainment—there's also an educational component involved, as the handlers are full of information on the creatures they tend to. The ranch allows you to see magnificent exotic creatures without having to travel halfway around the world.

For a unique family adventure, why not try out their 90-minute camel expedition through the scenic landscape, guided by friendly and knowledgeable experts. Kids will delight in the fact that feeding animals and birds is allowed and encouraged. For more information, check out their website: safariwilderness.com.

Giraffe Ranch in Dade City

Giraffe Ranch offers a wide range of animal encounters, including off-road vehicle rides, camel-back rides, or the option to roll around the park on a segway. This native wildlife preserve spans an impressive 47 acres and is home to a collection of exotic species from around the world, including:

- rhinos

- zebras

- ostriches

- monkeys

- pigs

- wild cats
- antelope
- pygmy hippos

Of course, the ranch's namesake creature, the gorgeous giraffe, is featured, too. It's a great place for families with kids of all ages. If Giraffe Ranch sounds like a good time, you can find out more by visiting them online at girafferanch.com.

Jungle Adventures in Christmas

If you want to travel into the past and see what Florida was like in its natural state, Jungle Adventures is the place to go. The area is home to numerous native Floridian animal species, including:

- Florida panthers
- black bears
- deer
- reptiles
- small mammals
- tropical birds

Visitors relish checking out their collection of baby alligators and other cute critters. Visitors can look forward to attending the Jumpin' Gator Jamboree, a live show where you can watch gators chomp down on slabs of raw meat, and you can also visit the Native American Village they've erected to show what life was like before settlers came to the area.

But that's not all! Jungle Adventures also offers a swamp cruise on the Green Gator River. Unlike the other parks, this one's focused on highlighting the natural flora and fauna of the Sunshine State, providing an authentic wildlife experience that goes way beyond typical theme park attractions, so if this adventure sounds like one that's right up your alley, make your way over to their website: jungleadventures.com/index.html (*Animal Encounters in Orlando*, n.d.).

Walks and Bike Rides

Orlando offers nature enthusiasts a variety of walking and cycling trails. Whether you're looking for a leisurely stroll, a smooth bike ride, or even a more challenging hike, the city and its surroundings have something for everyone, and best of all, You'll be able to capture stunning views of lakesides and hilltops.

Trails

Orlando's walking and cycling trails cater to a wide range of abilities, from easy walks perfect for a leisurely family outing to more challenging hikes that will satisfy the adventure seeker. Here are some top trails in and around Orlando:

- **Bear Creek Nature Trail:** A serene nature trail offering peaceful walking or cycling amid beautiful greenery and Florida palms right in Orlando. The trail isn't too long, but it's perfect for a leisurely family outing.

- **Big Tree Park:** The former home to one of the oldest and tallest trees in Florida, this park provides a unique opportunity to connect with ancient nature. Though the namesake Big Tree burned down over a decade ago, it's still worth a visit to walk its half-mile footpath that takes you through a swamp and links up with the bigger Cross Seminole Trail.

- **Black Bear Wilderness Loop Trail:** For the adventurous, this loop trail, located in Sanford, about a 35-minute drive from Orlando, takes visitors through a diverse ecosystem, offering a great chance to spot local wildlife, yes including bears. The 7-mile loop takes you through marshlands and serenity and is your best bet if you have your heart is set on seeing unfettered nature without having to venture too far from Orlando.

- **Black Hammock Trail:** The Black Hammock Wilderness Area in Oviedo, around 30 minutes from Orlando, is known for its scenic views of Lake Jessup and its tree-shaded path that'll help keep you cool as you peek over strawberry bushes harvested by the locals to make delicious pies and jams.

- **Cady Way Trail:** A popular paved urban trail, ideal for either cycling or walking, Cady Way connects Orlando with nearby Winter Park. The path gives residents and visitors alike a convenient way to exercise and navigate the city on foot.

- **Cypress Grove Park Loop:** A large, tranquil park on the shores of Lake Jasmine with a picturesque loop trail. This place is truly perfect for picnics or a peaceful afternoon stroll. There are also events held there frequently, so check local events calendars to see if there's anything going on during your visit.

- **Disney Wilderness Preserve:** Immerse yourself in the preserved natural beauty of Disney's conservation area, home to a variety of wildlife over 11,500 acres of tranquil Florida wilderness. This spot will prove to you that Disney isn't just about crowded parks and long lines.

- **Red Blaze Loop Trail at Hal Scott Preserve:** A six-mile loop that takes you through some beautiful wetland areas right near the University of Central Florida campus. This place is a great choice for a day hike, and there are a few other trails to choose from as well.

- **Kelly Park Loop Trail:** This 2.5-mile loop takes you through lush landscapes of a riverside bird and nature preserve. You can look forward to spotting waterfowl, turkeys, birds of prey, and more!

- **Lake Davis Park:** Featuring a beautiful paved urban walking trail that takes you around Lake Davis. The lake offers a relaxing atmosphere for a leisurely walk right in the heart of the city.

- **Lake Eola Park:** Enjoy a leisurely walk around this iconic downtown Orlando lake, surrounded by city views. You can find farmers' markets here on the weekends, and you can enjoy the dynamic urban landscape while relaxing with a picnic or even going on a swan boat ride! Make sure to visit the Thornton Park area located just on the other side of the lake.

- **Lake Underhill Park Loop:** A scenic loop around and across a bridge that stretches over Lake Underhill, this spot, which is located just east of the city, offers a peaceful escape right outside the heart of Orlando.

- **Orlando Urban Trail:** Explore the urban core of Orlando while enjoying a walk along this demarcated pedestrian and bike route that spans the city. The path goes right by a number of sites that you might want to visit, including the Science Center, the Museum of Art, and the stunning Mead Botanical Garden.

- **Pine Island East Loop Trail:** Traverse this 3.4-mile loop trail, which begins in the town of Hunter's Creek and gives you an inside look at the Everglades. While on your adventure, make sure to keep your eyes peeled for gators, wild turkeys, and deer.

- **Shadow Bay Loop Park:** Right in the shadow of nearby Universal Studios, this serene park, with a picturesque loop trail, offers visitors a quiet respite from all the hustle and bustle of the theme park. There are a few different walking trails to choose from, a variety of public athletic fields, and even a nearby campground where adventurous vacationers with tents and camping equipment or those traveling in RVs can book a night under the stars.

- **Split Oak Forest Wildlife & Environmental Area:** Discover the diverse wildlife and lush environment of this beautiful wetlands nature preserve, where you can observe species of native animals, including the gopher tortoise, the scrub-jay, and the Sherman's fox. Keep your eyes peeled for the famous split tree, an old oak that's split in half but lives on to this day.

- **The Seminole-Wekiva Trail:** A well-maintained 14-mile trail for cycling or walking that stretches far out into Orlando's suburbs, any section of this route can be the perfect path for vacationers who seek an easy and scenic outing. The trail takes you from Orlando through Altamonte Springs and all the way to Lake Mary (Sareen, 2023).

Did You Know?

Orlando boasts more than 100 parks (Gayatri, 2021), each one offering a unique natural experience. These parks and community centers provide a variety of enjoyable features, including nature trails, wide green spaces, and opportunities for sports and outdoor activities.

For a unique botanical experience, consider visiting the Harry P. Leu Gardens. This historical park and museum, located by Lake Rowena, is a hidden gem filled with tropical flowers and draped in Spanish moss. It's a tranquil oasis amidst the city's excitement, perfect for nature enthusiasts and those seeking a quieter side of Orlando.

Share Your Insights!

We'd love to hear from you! If you've explored the natural wonders of Orlando or have tips and insights to share, join the conversation. Use the hashtag #DiscoverOrlandoGuide on social media to connect with fellow travelers and outdoor enthusiasts. Share your favorite hiking spots, wildlife encounters, or any hidden gems you've uncovered in Orlando. Your insights could be just the inspiration someone needs to embark on their next Orlando adventure. So, don't hesitate— let's build a community of nature lovers and explorers right here in the heart of Florida. Your stories and tips are invaluable!

Are You Hungry Yet?

We've soaked up the sun and enjoyed the great outdoors, discovering the natural beauty Orlando has to offer. But what's a vacation without some delicious food to savor? In the next chapter, we'll take you on a culinary journey through Orlando, exploring the best bites the city has to offer. Get ready to tantalize your taste buds and satisfy your culinary cravings. Orlando's food scene is as diverse and exciting as its natural landscapes, so let's dig in and feast our way through The City Beautiful!

Chapter 5:

Restaurants and Food

Orlando isn't just a feast for the eyes and the soul—it's a feast for your taste buds, too! Beyond the enchanting theme parks and natural wonders, the city is a culinary playground where diverse flavors and delectable dishes await around every corner. From sizzling seafood to mouthwatering Cuban cuisine, Orlando's food scene is as diverse as its attractions.

In this chapter, we embark on a gastronomic journey through Orlando's vibrant culinary landscape. We'll explore the must-try foods that define the city's palate and guide you to the standout restaurants where you can savor them. Whether you're seeking budget-friendly bites, park food adventures, or the thrill of food festivals, we've got you covered.

Prepare to tantalize your taste buds and discover the delectable side of Orlando. From the bold, authentic flavors found on International Drive to the classy seafood-serving gems hidden within the city, from the rich heritage of Cuban cuisine to indulgent sweet treats, this chapter will satisfy your culinary cravings. Orlando's food culture is a reflection of its rich diversity, and we're here to help you navigate this mouthwatering array.

So, let's dive in and explore the culinary delights that make this city a food lover's paradise.

Must-Try Foods

Orlando boasts a culinary scene that's as diverse as its visitors. Whether you're an adventurous eater or someone who prefers familiar flavors, the city offers a wide range of dining experiences. In this section, we'll clue you in on all the essentials of finding good grub around Orlando, starting with the delectable offerings along International Drive.

International Drive: A World of Flavors

International Drive, often simply referred to by locals as I-Drive, is a food lover's paradise where a global smorgasbord awaits. This bustling thoroughfare is lined with an array of restaurants and eateries, each offering a unique taste of international cuisine. From Latin American to Asian cuisine to European and American standbys, I-Drive is a melting pot of flavors.

Types of Cuisine You Can Expect to Find on I-Drive:

- **American classics and international fusion:** For those who crave all-American fare, you can't go wrong with hearty burgers, steaks, and barbecue. You'll be happy to spot old stand-bys and chains like The Cheesecake Factory, TG Friday's, and IHOP, but some of the best bites are to be found in the local, independent businesses that fry up delicious breakfasts and juicy burgers. Plus, there's a whole bunch of places that serve up standard far, plus exciting small plates with international flair.

- **Latin American specialties:** Savor the fiery and flavorful dishes from countries like Mexico, Cuba, Puerto Rico, and the Dominican Republic. Enjoy classics like ropa vieja, empanadas, mofongo, churrasco, tacos, and birria, giving you a taste of the Caribbean, and Central and South America.

- **Asian fare:** Dive into the world of Chinese buffets, sushi, dim sum, and ramen. You'll find a diverse range of Asian cuisine in Orlando, from Japanese to Korean to Chinese and Thai.

- **European cuisine:** Experience the rich flavors of Europe with Italian pasta, classic French bistro fare, and delectable small bites inspired by Spanish tapas and Greek mezze. The options are varied and run the whole range from affordable pizzerias and family dining spots to more refined locales that are perfect for a romantic dinner for two.

Standout Restaurants Near International Drive

American Classics and International Fusion

- **The Diner:** A great choice for fresh, homemade breakfast, brunch & lunch options, visitors of all ages go crazy for simple but well-prepared dishes such as chicken and waffles, decadent stuffed french toast, and delightful eggs benedict.

- **Maple Street Biscuit Company:** If you're looking for a killer brunch, look no further than O-Town's own Maple Street Biscuit Company. With a menu packed with whimsically-named breakfast options, you'll be writing home to friends and relatives about the Southern-inflected culinary flare demonstrated in dishes like the bluegrass grits bow, side fried chicken, and the sticky maple chicken-n-biscuits platter.

- **Lazy Dog Restaurant and Bar:** American comfort food served straight up without any fuss. This casual stop is great for families and is reasonably priced. Soups, burgers, and salads—what else do you need? But that's not all: If you're feeling fancy or want to taste some international flavors too, they've got you covered with options like lettuce wraps, a Japanese-inspired Katu chicken sandwich to die for, and rare tuna encrusted in sesame seeds.

- **The Whiskey:** With bar food and small bites inspired by their namesake drink, whether you're looking for a great burger, piled-high nachos, or just want to have a quick drink, this place is great for whiskey lovers; plus they've got live music to boot!

- **Cafe Tu Tu Tango:** If eclectic fusion fare sounds right up your alley, you might consider stepping into this artsy restaurant where you can savor small plates inspired by various cultures all while enjoying live entertainment. Their dynamite shrimp is true to its name, and their Cuban sliders and fish tacos serve as a testament to the greatness of Floridian cuisine, offering any tourists in doubt huge heaps of culinary delight.

- **Chef Art Smith's Homecomin':** If you're seeking out some of that good Southern cooking, Homecomin'—a restaurant by Chef Art Smith, is one of your best bets on I-Drive. Make sure you come with a hearty appetite, as the servings are quite large. Old stand-bys such as fried chicken, fried catfish, and freshly baked biscuits are the highlights here. For all you health-conscious travelers out there: Don't worry; they've got plenty of vegetables, too. Make sure to have a reservation well in advance if you plan to visit Homecomin' during your Orlando vacation.

- **Whisper Creek Farm: The Kitchen:** Located at the JW Mariott hotel, this place serves farm-to-table American fare and is a great place for classic steaks and chops and oysters with a modern twist. Meat lovers will love their smoked short rib or glazed skirt steak, while veg-hounds will be happy to see their wide range of fresh produce that's all grown locally and concocted into carefully crafted, hearty entrees and light, refreshing salads.

- **Dixie Belle's Cafe:** A hidden gem serving classic Southern breakfasts and brunches. If you've got a hankering for some good old biscuits and gravy, this is

From chicken-fried steak to pancakes and perfectly molded waffles with dollops syrup, they've got just about anything you e, and it's pretty affordable to boot. Hey,)u just want to go to a regular old diner ? "normal" yet exceptional food, and for those times—Dixie Belle's is the place.

Latin American Specialties

- **El Patron Restaurante:** This Mexican taqueria and restaurant will have your senses activated with busts of authentic flavors from south of the border in a modern, refined setting. Whether you've got a hankering for a snack of elote and a few micheladas or want to go all-in on a *plato* filled with *carne asada an*d fresh *tortillas* they've got you covered. The best part? They also offer an unlimited lunch buffet—so if you want to come out the other side of this fresh-mex experience stuffed to the brim like a *chile relleno,* get in that line and go for it! I promise that you won't be disappointed.

- **Q'Kenan Restaurant:** If the savory, delicious tastes of Venezuela are appealing to you—you might just find a delicious meal at this Caracas-inspired cafe that boasts a menu of delicious typical dishes. Stand-out dishes include the *arepas,* shredded chicken, mixed grill, and delicious cocktails. For dessert, why not order a *tres leches* cake?

- **Pio Pio Restaurant:** If you're a fan of South American cuisine, Pio Pio offers up a menu filled with Colombian and Peruvian classics that'll fill your stomach and your soul. Offering delicious *platos tipicos,* featuring grilled and roasted meats alongside fresh vegetables and rice and beans, there are also, of course, a wide range of soups and *empanadas* to choose from.

Cuban Culinary Delights

Orlando's culinary landscape is heavily influenced by its vibrant Cuban community. The city is home to some outstanding Cuban restaurants where you can indulge in the flavors of this Caribbean island. Whatever places you end up dining at, make sure to keep your eyes peeled for these mouth-watering traditional plates.

Popular Cuban Dishes

- **Ropa Vieja:** Shredded beef simmered in a tomato-based sauce with peppers and onions. While this dish isn't just Cuban and is something you'll find all around Latin America; it's something you have to try!

- **Cuban Sandwich:** A classic sandwich featuring roast pork, ham, Swiss cheese, pickles, and mustard on Cuban bread. It's not from Cuba, but from right here in Florida, making it a true Cuban-American classic!

- **Tostones:** Twice-fried smashed green plantains, typically served as a side dish or snack. It's not sweet like its older cousin, *maduros,* but instead is a savory, healthy alternative to french fries.

- **Yuca con Mojo:** Starchy cassava root served with a garlicky citrus sauce. It'll put that mojo back in your step!

Where to Satisfy Your Cuban Cravings

- **Sofrito Latin Cafe:** If the authentic tastes of Cuba are what you're after, and you're also looking for a quick, casual spot for a great brunch with bold flavors, this spot just might be what you're after. As I already mentioned, the *Cubano* sandwich itself is a Florida-born specialty. If you haven't had one before in the Sunshine State, the place where it was created, it's a must-try. With a wide variety of *platos tipicos,* not just from Cuba but also from all across Latin America, such as *pernil* roast pork, *lomo saltado,* and salted pork loin on the menu, as well as a vast arrange of sandwiches, *empanadas,* and other delicacies, you're bound to find something that tastes good at this Latin-infused spot.

- **Havana's Cuban Cuisine:** Floridian cuisine as a whole owes much to the cuisine of Cuba and the Caribbean. If tasting the authentic flavors of Cuba is on your Florida checklist, you're going to want to make sure to put Havana's down at the top. Offering traditional dishes such as *mofongo, camaguey, ropa vieja,* and, *churrasco*—this is truly the place to go if you want to experience the authentic flavors of the reclusive island nation located just 90 miles from Florida's Southern coast.

- **Black Bean Deli:** If you want to try traditional Cuban food but aren't a fan of heavy, oil-laden dishes, Black Bean Deli is known as a healthier choice, offering traditional dishes, as well as some more modern-infused lighter fare, including salads, and fresh vegan and vegetarian options. The place is a long-time local favorite where you can savor authentic Cuban sandwiches and other Cuban staples in setting.

- **Havana Bistro & Cafe:** Known for its *carne* stewed meat and perfectly executed *ropa vieja*, straight up perfectly executed this spot serves up piping-hot Cuban dishes in a no-frills setting. It's a great choice for a quick lunch while out exploring Orlando, and they offer snacks, like empanadas and fresh juices, too—so there's no pressure to sit down and stay a while.

- **Versailles Restaurant:** If you want to see what an old-school Cuban-American cafe looks like, you've got to go and check out this spot, which is known for its lively atmosphere and extensive menu. This restaurant is a must-visit for Cuban food enthusiasts. You won't find any fancy decor or white tablecloths here, just authentic Cuban cuisine served straight up without any of the fuss and frills found in finer-dining establishments. Don't come to this spot expecting a sit-down multi-course affair. It's a great spot for on-the-go empanadas, delicious sandwiches, and lunch platters bursting with flavorful rice and meat.

European Cuisine

- **Mia's Italian Kitchen:** If you're looking for heaping portions of Italian-American fare, you could just go to the Olive Garden—but know that there's a better option right around the corner on I-Drive. At Mia's, you'll be swimming in sauce like a true *goombah*. Everyone knows some of the best Sicilian flavors are to be found in New York and New Jersey, but hey, like all of us, these folks eventually want to retire too, and where do they make their way from the blistering winds up North other than straight to Florida? With classic comfort plated like chicken parmigiana and baked rigatoni, you'll feel like you're part of the family in this welcoming *ristorante*.

- **La Boucherie:** French bistro-fare might not be the first thing that comes to your mind when thinking about the vast array of dining options in Florida, but this place is truly not to be missed. Whether you're looking for a classic steak frites or a fresh salad, there's something for everyone on this non-fussy French-inspired menu. While they've got some fancy things like foie gras, the majority of the menu is composed of simple yet delicious combinations of roasted meats and fish with delectable fresh veggies.

Asian Fare

- **Susuru:** You may have seen this Izakaya-style Japanese spot featured on TikTok, as it's a popular spot just 15 minutes from Disney and is much lauded for its delicious food and authentic ambiance. Focusing on small plates, like grilled yakitori and other meat skewers, this place is a great locale to kick back and have some beers while noshing on a variety of small plates or bigger entrees if you want. From rice bowls to ramen—they have it all.

- **YH Seafood Clubhouse:** If you're looking for great Chinese food in Orlando, look no further than this spot. Tucked away in a strip mall, this unassuming spot doesn't give any clues to its flavor-packed menu on the exterior, but once you step inside, you're transported into a world of flavor beyond your wildest imagination. Focusing on Cantonese staples, their menu features a wide variety of *dim sum* small plates as well as family-style meat, seafood, and veggie entrees. This place is considered one of the best Chinese restaurants in Orlando, so making a reservation is wise practice.

- **Boil Spot:** Korean hotpot promises a world of flavor and an unforgettable hands-on dining experience. If you haven't tried it before, I seriously urge you to try! With a wide variety of fresh meats and veggies, the helpful serves will make sure you have all you need to craft a delectable meal from the comfort of your table as you steep their fresh ingredients in a fully customizable broth that'll warm your soul and light your taste buds ablaze. The best part? It's all you can eat! There are options for a hot pot menu or a hot pot plus BBQ menu.

- **Kungfu Kitchen:** This New York transplant street food-inspired place serves up dumplings and soups in a casual setting, making it the perfect place to stop for a delicious lunch on a rainy off-season day exploring Orlando. With a menu featuring *bao*, soup dumplings, noodle soups, and meat, seafood, and vegetarian entrees, you're bound to find something delicious while you sip a pot of hot jasmine tea.

The Seafood Scene

As a city in close proximity to both the Atlantic Coast and the Gulf of Mexico, Orlando serves some of the freshest seafood in Florida. Wherever you choose to dine during your trip, from upscale seafood restaurants to laid-back coastal shacks, there's a multitude of options to indulge in the ocean's bounty. There are a few dishes in particular that I'd really recommend you try if you're a lover of seafood.

Must-Try Seafood Dishes

- **Florida Grouper:** Try this local favorite, often prepared with a light seasoning and served grilled or blackened. It might be an ugly bottom-feeder, but it tastes like pure magic!

- **Conch Fritters:** Enjoy this Bahamian specialty, often served with a zesty dipping sauce. The conch is very well known for its distinctive shell. *Who knew you could eat it too?*

- **Stone Crab Claws:** If you're visiting during crab season, which is typically mid-October through the beginning of May, don't miss the opportunity to savor some of these sweet claws.

- **Shrimp and Grits:** A Southern staple, this dish combines succulent shrimp with creamy grits and a flavorful sauce. It's great for a lazy breakfast or brunch served up Southern-style!

Where to Find the Freshest Catch

- **The Boathouse:** Serving up Florida staples like grilled Mahi-Mahi, this seafood-lovers paradise offers a pristine raw bar and some New England-inspired fare, too, including sweet-boiled Maine lobsters that you can slather in buttery sauce. As you may have guessed, the focus of the menu is the offering of the sea; however—for all you meat lovers out there, don't worry; they offer a decent fillet mignon, too! Whatever floats your boat, you'll always find a seat at the table at the Boathouse.

- **192 Crab and Lobster:** If you love sport and seafood, this place is for you! Aside from the fresh catch on offer, this spot has a great bar that features numerous TVs broadcasting the best in sports games. Who doesn't love watching NCAA finals while gnawing on some crab's legs? As you may have surmised, this is a casual spot, and the prices are reasonable, too. One thing to note is that gratuity is included, so for those of you traveling from abroad and are U.S.-tip challenged, don't worry about calculations; they'll tack it onto your bill for you.

- **Ocean Prime:** Now, let's talk about a place that's great for a romantic night out or an important business dinner. Ocean Prime is a top-quality seafood restaurant and steakhouse that combines elegance with a diverse menu of seafood options. It's definitely not the most affordable option around, but it more than makes up for it in the refined menu offering and exquisite service. The menu's nothing that's going to surprise you, but you'll find that it's all cooked to perfection. From creamy lobster bisque to perfectly executed Chilean sea bass to an exquisite surf and turf, with surprising side options like *jalapeño au gratin*, you'll find that this place, while more traditional, is not without its own brand of innovative twists on steakhouse stand-bys.

Sweet Treats Galore

No meal is complete without a sweet ending, and Orlando delivers on the dessert front. Whether you're a fan of bakeries or dessert shops, the city offers a delightful array of sugary delights that will satisfy any sweet tooth. Here are the ones you must try before leaving:

- **Key Lime Pie:** This tangy and sweet dessert is a Florida classic. You can even find a boxed-up frozen version to fly home within many local shops, or you can air mail it to your sweetheart or jealous friends, keeping tabs on your Orlando thrills via Instagram.

- **Cupcakes:** From classic red velvet to creative flavor combinations, Orlando's cupcake shops have it all. Though some say these treats were just a trend, Orlando's storied cupcake emporiums show us that they're here to stay!

- **Ice Cream:** Cool down with a scoop of homemade ice cream in a variety of flavors. From classic flavors to the exotic realms of inexplicable flavor combinations, there's something for everyone in Orlando, whether you're a cone person or a cup die-hard.

- **Doughnuts:** Enjoy a wide range of doughnut varieties, from glazed to gourmet. They may not look like much at the surface level, but I can assure you—Orlando has some of the best doughnuts in the world.

- **Cheesecake:** Dive into rich, creamy cheesecakes with a plethora of toppings and flavors. Just make sure not to leave those extra slices in your car, as you'll be in for a nasty surprise once they get sun-baked and quickly begin to spoil, potentially sneaking their way around your rental car's incidental coverage.

Bakeries and Dessert Spots to Visit

- **The Glass Knife:** Whether you've got a sweet tooth for cakes, doughnuts, or exquisitely crafted *macarons*, this place has some of the best desserts in Orlando. And the best part is that they have coffee, sandwiches, and salads, too!

- **Gideon's Bakehouse:** Famous for its cookies, cakes, and amazing flavored coffees, Gideon's is a must-visit for dessert enthusiasts looking for a sweet pit stop near Disney.

In-Park Food Options

Orlando's theme parks are not only playgrounds for thrilling rides and magical experiences but also havens for unique and delicious internationally-lauded dining adventures. From character-themed dishes to budget-friendly bites, the parks offer a culinary journey that complements the excitement of all the thrilling attractions.

Unique Meals in the Magic Kingdom and Beyond

Character-Themed Dishes

One of the best parts of Orlando's theme parks is the opportunity to enjoy meals inspired by beloved characters. From whimsical desserts to hearty meals, these character-themed dishes found at Disney add an extra layer of magic to your park experience.

- Mickey ice cream bar
- Mickey waffles
- Mickey pretzel
- Mickey beignet

Eating on a Budget in the Magic Kingdom and Universal Studios

Budget-Friendly Tips

While the appeal of theme park dining is undeniable, it can be really expensive! This makes it crucial to do your research in advance and arm yourself with the tools to navigate your way to budget-friendly options without compromising on taste. Here are some tips and spots to enjoy affordable yet tasty meals.

Disney

Dining in-park can be expensive, and it's recommended to bring plenty of snacks and maybe to consider packing sandwiches and other more substantial fare. But let's face it, the appeal of dining in-park is undeniable. This is why it's important to know that there are some reasonable options to be found at Disney. Here are my top choices for the best budget-friendly dining options:

- **Pecos Bill Tall Tale Inn and Cafe** at the Magic Kingdom in Frontierland
- **Columbia Harbour House** at the Magic Kingdom
- **Casey's Corner** at the Magic Kingdom
- **Kabuki Cafe** at EPCOT
- **Via Napoli** at EPCOT
- **Flame Tree Barbecue** at Animal Kingdom
- **Backlot Express** at Hollywood Studios
- **ABC Commissary** at Hollywood Studios

Universal

- **Mel's Drive-In** at Universal Studios

- **Louie's Italian Restaurant** at Universal
- **Bread Box Handcrafted Sandwiches** at Universal CityWalk
- **Hot Dog Hall of Fame** at Universal CityWalk
- **Croissant Moon Bakery** at Universal Islands of Adventure
- **Three Broomsticks** at the Wizarding World of Harry Potter in Universal Islands of Adventure

Whether you're dining with Disney characters or seeking budget-friendly snacks at Universal, Orlando's theme parks cater to every palate and pocket. While your tab can easily rack up if you dine out every day, don't be afraid to check out the delicious in-park food options as you explore the magical world of these iconic attractions.

Food Events

Orlando's culinary scene isn't confined to traditional restaurants; it also extends to a whole range of vibrant food festivals that offer a delectable array of flavors for every palate. From the renowned Epcot Food and Wine Festival to local foodie gatherings and the allure of food trucks, Orlando's food-focused events are a feast for the senses.

Epcot International Food and Wine Festival

The Epcot International Food and Wine Festival, which typically runs from late July through late November, is a

93

...s-long gastronomic extravaganza that takes place annually at EPCOT, offering hungry visitors a global culinary journey right in the heart of Walt Disney World. See the entry in Chapter 3: The Magic of Theme Parks for more information about what kind of international treats this foodie haven has to offer.

Fall Food Festivals

As more mild autumn temperatures descend upon Orlando, they bring with them some tantalizing aromas and flavors through a series of annual festivals that beckon food enthusiasts from all corners.

From the fiery spice of jerk chicken to the savory allure of crackling pork skin, each festival becomes a culinary journey, where the rich and diverse flavors of fall meld seamlessly with the spirit of communal celebration. In this section, we embark on a gastronomic adventure through the fall food festivals of October and November, savoring the unique and mouthwatering offerings that grace the tables of these annual gatherings.

October

- **Annual Swinetoberfest:** At the Ravenous Pig restaurant in Winter Park in early October.

- **Orlando Jerk Festival:** Held at varying locations each year.

November

- **Annual Fall Fiesta in the Park:** Held at Lake Eola Park in early November.

- **A Taste of Thornton Park:** Held at Thornton Park in early November.

- **Walt Disney World Swan And Dolphin Food and Wine Classic:** Held at the Swan & Dolphin Hotel at EPCOT.

- **FusionFest:** Held in Downtown Orlando the Saturday and Sunday after Thanksgiving.

Food Trucks in the City Beautiful

Orlando's food truck scene is a great way to sample the city's diverse culinary offerings without spending too much. These mobile kitchens offer a delightful array of dishes, from gourmet street food to creative fusions. Here are some tips on the best ways to spot and track down these rolling delights:

World Food Truck Park in Kissimmee

Checking out Central Florida's only designated food truck park, where multiple trucks come together to offer a vast array of bold flavors, is one of your best bets for finding good eats around the city. The street-food oases you'll find at World Food Truck Park are perfect for sampling a variety of flavors in one convenient location.

From burgers to tacos to Puerto Rican, Dominican, Cuban, Salvadoran, and Venezuelan specialties, you'll be jam-packed with flavor-bursting grub by the time you make your way through the place. Here's a list of what kind of food options you can expect to find from the more than 60 independently owned and operated trucks you'll find here:

- desserts of all kinds, including ice cream, snow cones, funnel cakes, waffles, and fresh fruits

- coffee, fresh squeezed fruit juices, smoothies, shakes, and boba

- Latin American cuisine from all different countries

- fried and grilled fresh seafood

- sushi

- Chinese

- pizza

- burgers

- wraps and kebabs.

- a wide array of delicious, authentic street foods and fusion creations from all over the world

Pro Tips For Finding Affordable Eats Across the City

Outside of the delectable dining options you can find at World Food Truck Park, use platforms like Roaming Hunger to discover the current locations of food trucks in Orlando. This dynamic tool helps you plan your culinary adventure based on real-time information. Some neighborhoods and events attract food trucks regularly, so keep an eye out for these local hotspots.

Did You Know?

In the late 1800s, Orlando was known as the capital of Florida oranges. This all ended when the deep freeze of 1895 brought about a frosty end to this prosperous grove-filled era, forcing farming families to relocate further south.

Today, Florida's orange legacy lives on, with 569,000 acres of groves producing over 50 million boxes of citrus annually (Westgate Resorts, 2023). Today, visitors can still experience the history of Orlando citrus cultivation at The Showcase of Citrus, where you can pick your own oranges and even ride a real monster truck.

Share Your Insights!

We want to hear about your experience of the vibrant flavors of Orlando and provide a platform for you to share your culinary escapades using our dedicated hashtag, #OrlandoFoodExplorer! Whether it's a hidden gem you stumbled upon, a mouthwatering dish you can't stop thinking about, or a budget-friendly eatery that surprised you, let your fellow foodies in on the delicious details. Your insights will be the secret ingredient for others seeking a taste of Orlando's diverse food scene. Join the conversation, and let's create a delectable community of Orlando culinary adventurers!

Ready For More Activities Yet? Let's Go!

Now that we've savored the diverse and delectable flavors of Orlando, it's time to have some family fun! In the upcoming chapter, we'll explore activities that cater to all ages, ensuring memorable moments for everyone. From thrilling attractions to serene escapes, Orlando has a myriad of experiences awaiting your discovery. So, buckle up for the family fun time ahead and get ready for some tips on how to create enduring vacation memories in the heart of the Sunshine State!

Chapter 6:

Family Fun Time

Orlando isn't just about burning through your life savings at the big theme parks while making your kids' dreams come true—it also offers visitors a plethora of free off-park family adventures, all just waiting to be discovered. In this chapter, we'll unveil the secrets to navigating Disney and Universal, as well as clue you into some other types of wholesome, low-key fun in the area.

Parks for Kids

Are you, like many, traveling to Orlando to visit the theme parks with the little ones in tow? You can make the most of your family escapade with these invaluable tips for navigating the big theme parks with ease:

- **Toddlers in tow? You pay nothing.** Children under three enjoy free entry to most of Orlando's theme parks and water attractions.

- **Utilize the rider swap option on rides (Child Switch Pass).** For attractions with height restrictions, use the rider swap service offered by numerous rides. One parent waits with the little one while the other enjoys the ride, then swap roles for a hassle-free experience.

- **Consider priority passes.** Minimize wait times for your little one by securing priority passes for must-see theme park rides. Universal Orlando Resort offers the Universal Express™ Pass, while SeaWorld offers Quick Queue® Unlimited for front-of-the-line access. LEGOLAND provides the Fastrack service in Unlimited and 3-pack options.

- **Get the apps.** The My Disney Experience app offers the free Disney Genie Service, helping you optimize your time at Walt Disney World Resort. It also features a paid Disney Genie+ Lightning Lane Entrance for over 40 attractions and an Individual Lightning Lane Entrance for highly sought-after rides.

- **Bring snacks with you.** Keep hunger tantrums at bay by having a stash of snacks ready. Let's face it: Dining in-park can be expensive, so pack snacks and sandwiches, especially if you have allergies or special diets or if you just have picky eaters.

- **Navigate the parks counterclockwise.** Large crowds tend to move together, and studies have shown that the majority of Orlando theme park visitors meander in a clockwise direction through the attractions (*Orlando Theme Park Tips & Tricks to Save Your Sanity*, 2016). This means that by going in the direction of foot traffic, you may be able to save time and avoid big crowds and traffic jams.

- **Utilize family-friendly amenities.** Every theme park provides designated areas for diaper changes, nursing stations, and more. Familiarize yourself with these facilities before your visit, and take advantage of free maps and guides.

- **Visit dedicated "lands" for toddler-friendly rides.** Visit the parks' "lands" for all the best kiddie rides—research age and height restrictions on the theme park websites to find rides suitable for toddlers. Check with attraction operators for specific ride details.

- **Save Harry Potter for late in the day.** If you're planning to explore the Wizarding World of Harry Potter at Universal, save it for the evening when crowds tend to thin out. Avoid pricey souvenir wands at Universal Studios, and consider budget-friendly alternatives if you're a Harry Potter-head on a budget.

By following these tips, your family can make the most of Orlando's theme parks with a toddler in tow, creating happy memories for the whole family.

Learn and Play

Orlando offers a wealth of educational and entertaining attractions for families, where kids can have fun while expanding their horizons. Here are some of the top science, art, and history-related places to explore.

Science

Kennedy Space Center

Take your family on an out-of-this-world adventure at the Kennedy Space Center. This awe-inspiring space hub offers a glimpse into the world of space exploration. You can explore the Visitor Complex with exhibits on space history, astronaut encounters and even watch rocket launches streamed on closed circuit TV from the nearby Cape Canaveral launch site.

Special events like astronaut Q&A sessions are held throughout the year. There's also a special Astronaut Training Experience for both kids and adults sponsored by weapons manufacturer Lockheed Martin. In the four- to five-hour sessions, visitors will have a unique hands-on training experience for a mission to Mars based on the program that real astronauts undergo in preparation for planned missions to the Red Planet.

Ticket prices, of course, can vary depending on the experience you choose, and there is a wide array of options. The current entry fee for a standard one-day pass to the visitors center is $75, with $10 off for kids 11 and under.

Orlando Science Center

Fuel your child's curiosity at the Orlando Science Center, a hub for interactive learning. With hands-on exhibits and engaging displays, kids can explore various aspects of science, from the human body to the cosmos. It's an ideal place for young minds to have fun while gaining knowledge. *The best part?* There are even activities and exhibits suitable for infants and toddlers!

At the DinoDigs exhibit, your kids will have the chance to participate in a realistic excavation for dinosaur bones while viewing a vast array of prehistoric sea and land creatures. At Our Planet, Our Solar System, young visitors are able to explore other planets while learning facts about outer space through a series of interactive displays.

For younger children, up to seven, the KidsTown area holds a whole bunch of surprises and opportunities for discovery through play. A new exhibit called Life is slated to open in Spring 2024 and will focus on animals and their natural habitats. Tickets for an adult entry are $24, $18 for kids 11 and under, and under-twos entering for free. Senior citizens and students get a discounted rate of $22.

Art and History

Aside from the Science Center, Orlando boasts a number of other museums suitable for children. While they may not find the same thrills that you do at some of these more high-brow spots, they're still worth a visit, especially on a low-key off-day or if there's inclement weather that prevents you from enjoying outdoor attractions. Here are some of the best choices for families looking to show their kids a bit of culture and art:

Fort Christmas Historical Park

This park takes you back in time with its unique collection of historical buildings and artifacts, including a re-created fort that was originally built on the grounds of the park way back in 1837. Families can also look forward to checking out a series of pioneer homes and a traditional "cracker" house, the simple shelters that the first settlers built when they arrived in Florida. There's also a playground on-site, making this place one of my top choices for a family-friendly day out filled with history and fun.

The Orlando Museum of Art

This beloved Orlando institution boasts a diverse collection of art from the Americas and Africa, including some family-friendly exhibitions. Specifically for kids, there are monthly Art Adventures, which allows children to get hands-on with arts and crafts. The program is suitable for kids from two to ten years old. The sessions take place on select Friday mornings, so make sure to check their events calendar. There are also Art in the Afternoons arts and crafts sessions for kids seven and up, which also take place on select Fridays throughout the month.

The Albin Polasek Museum

This museum and sculpture garden features the work of Czech artist Albin Polasek. The historic home offers a unique blend of art and outdoor exploration in a beautiful sculpture garden. While there aren't any exhibitions specifically for children, they'll love spotting tropical birds and observing the local flora as you make your way through the garden's winding path. It's a great spot for a quick visit after lunch visit. Entry is $12 for a regular adult admission, with kids under four entering for free. K-12 students and seniors enter for $10.

The Orlando Fire Museum

This small museum, housed in an old firehouse in the Loch Haven Park area of Orlando, includes a number of ornate, antique fire trucks, among other treasures and relics, such as antique fireboxes and firefighter's clothing and tools. While they're not allowed to slide down it themselves due to safety and liability concerns, kids will love seeing the original fireman's pole, which has been fitted with a mannequin, posed as if he's descending down to the lower level to take action.

Animal Encounters

Kids love animals, and Orlando has several zoos and aquariums that provide unique and educational experiences. At Gatorland, which we already covered in detail in Chapter 3, you can get up close and personal with alligators, crocodiles, and other wildlife. Of course, SeaWorld is always a favorite and is also featured in detail in Chapter 3

If you still haven't had your fill of animals or have an aspiring young zoologist or veterinarian in the family, there are a few more great options for seeing wild animals in and around Orlando that the young ones will love!

The Central Florida Zoo & Botanical Gardens

This place offers a compelling mix of exotic animals, including endangered species, amid its beautiful gardens featuring a wide range of native Florida trees and plants. But there's more: Visitors can take a ride on their miniature train called The Champion, which takes you on a wild, adventurous ride all throughout the zoo. The train itself is a quarter-scale replica of a real Atlantic Coast Railroad steam engine train. Admission prices can vary depending on the season, but you can expect to pay around $24 for an adult entry and $20 or so for kids. The train ride costs $5 for all.

Discovery Cove

If your dream is to swim with dolphins, this is the best place to do it in Central Florida. While there are plenty of snorkeling opportunities to be found on the coasts, Discovery Cove is right outside Orlando in Kissimmee, making it an easy choice for those seeking an ocean-like experience without the long drive. The place is an all-inclusive day resort, so keep in mind that while the tickets might seem a bit pricy compared to other attractions, this isn't any regular old attraction.

Guests are encouraged to make it a full-day experience, starting with a delicious breakfast, which is included, along with a delicious lunch and unlimited snacks and beverages throughout the day. Kids will love playing in the pristine sands of the resort's artificial beaches and gentle wading pools. They're also able to touch, play with, and feed tropical birds at the on-site aviary. They'll also have a chance to meet armadillos and sloths! Prices can vary throughout the year, and there are a wide variety of booking options, some including hotel reservations in addition to entry to SeaWorld and Aquatica.

Jungle Adventures Nature Park and Zoo

If you're looking for some classic Florida-style family wildlife entertainment, Jungle Adventures just might be right up your alley. With both wild animal shows and swamp tours, what's not to love? Aside from the Florida Panter that lives on the grounds, they also have a few smaller wildcats, a number of deer, and a wide range of small mammals, reptiles, and a vast collection of exotic birds. You won't want to miss their gator jamboree feeding sessions. Admission prices can vary throughout the year, but you can expect to pay around $25 for each adult, $20 for seniors, and $16 or so for kids.

Smooth Waters Wildlife Park

With over 50 species of native and exotic animals, the exhibits at this smaller, family-run zoo not only entertain but also inspire young minds while promoting ecological conservation and emphasizing taking good care of the critters housed there. You'll find gators here, in addition to tortoises and a number of other amazing reptiles. The place actually operates as an animal sanctuary, and the emphasis is on learning how to properly care for animals, not just showing off their unique characteristics to visitors. If you're lucky, they might even let you hold a baby alligator! If you're looking for a more personalized up-close experience with these creatures, Smooth Waters is your best bet, as their kind staff will guide you through their unique collection of amazing animals with care and compassion for nature! Adult entry to this homespun zoo is $10 for adults and $5 for kids.

More Fun Ideas

When you're in Orlando with your family, it's not just about theme parks and museums. There are plenty of other activities that provide wholesome entertainment for everyone. Here, I'll run you through a few of them.

Dinner Shows

Orlando is home to a variety of family-friendly dinner shows that offer a unique combination of dining and entertainment. These shows are not only worth the money, in my humble opinion, but also create lasting memories for your family. At places like Medieval Times and Pirates Dinner Adventure, you can enjoy vibrant performances and delicious food at the same time, making for a colorful experience that kids and adults will love.

Go-Karts and Racing

For families with a need for speed, Orlando offers thrilling go-kart experiences that are sure to get your adrenaline pumping. Places like Andretti Indoor Karting & Games and I-Drive NASCAR provide go-kart racing that's suitable for all ages. Whether you're a beginner or a seasoned driver, these tracks offer exciting challenges and a chance to test your racing skills in a safe environment.

Mini-Golf

Miniature golf is a classic family pastime, and Orlando has some of the best mini-golf courses in the country. Places like

Pirate's Cove Adventure Golf and Congo River Golf offer not only challenging courses but also immersive themes that transport you to different worlds. These are perfect spots for some friendly family competition.

Outdoor Adventures

Orlando's warm and sunny climate invites outdoor activities that the whole family can enjoy. The more popular water parks, such as Aquatica and Adventure Island, provide a refreshing escape from the Florida heat, featuring thrilling water slides and lazy rivers. Nature trails like the West Orange Trail or Shingle Creek Regional Park offer opportunities for hiking and exploring the natural beauty of Florida. Whether you're looking for a splash or a scenic stroll, Orlando has outdoor options for every family.

The unique activities found throughout Orlando and Central Florida complement the theme park-centric experience, offering a diverse range of cultural and amusement options for families visiting the area. So, on your trip, make sure to venture beyond the usual attractions and explore the city's wide range of family-friendly fun!

Did You Know?

Orlando is home to one of the world's most unique McDonald's locations. Known as the "Epic McD," this enormous fast-food joint covers a whopping 19,000 square feet (Westgate Resorts, 2023), making it one of the largest McDonald's restaurants on the planet. As you walk through its doors, you'll immediately notice that this McDonald's offers much more than just your favorite fast-food items.

Inside, the "Epic McD" boasts a staggering array of over 100 arcade games (Westgate Resorts, 2023), providing endless entertainment for visitors of all ages. If you're in the mood for a fun-filled family outing or just want to unleash your inner gamer, this McDonald's is the place to be.

The menu at this extraordinary McDonald's goes beyond the ordinary. While you'll find all the classic McDonald's offerings you love, it also features some surprising additions not typically associated with the fast-food giant. If you're feeling adventurous, you can sample items like pizza and pasta, adding a unique twist to your fast-food experience. So, when you're in Orlando and looking for a one-of-a-kind McDonald's adventure, the "Epic McD" is ready to serve you an unforgettable meal and gaming experience.

Share Your Insights!

Now, it's your turn to share your kid-friendly escapades and insights! Whether you've uncovered a fantastic off-park attraction or local playground, explored a unique museum, or had a blast at a family dinner show, we want to hear about your adventures.

Using the hashtag #DiscoverOrlandoGuide, share your stories, recommendations, and tips for making the most of Orlando with your little ones. Your experiences and insights can be a source of inspiration for other families looking to create magical moments in Orlando.

Let's connect through the joy and laughter of our kids as they explore the wonders of this incredible city. Share your family's Orlando adventures and help others discover the best kid-friendly experiences this city has to offer. We can't wait to hear your tales of vacation vibrancy and adventure!

Sick of the Kids Yet? It's Date Night Time!

From family outings filled with laughter to heartwarming moments spent with your little ones, Orlando has proven to be an unforgettable family destination. But as the sun sets, a new adventure awaits—the perfect date night. It's time to explore how Orlando can be the perfect backdrop for a week-long romantic retreat, or a date night to be remembered, and a well-deserved break from family activities and the dizzying pace of the big attractions.

Chapter 7:

Love in Orlando

Orlando, a city known for thrilling adventures and family-friendly attractions, often evokes images of joyous laughter and carefree moments. Yet, beneath its playful exterior, Orlando holds secrets that have the power to ignite the flames of love and seduce your partner. As the sun sets over the enchanting city, it unveils moments of unbridled passion, where lovers can bask in the beauty the city has to offer.

In the heart of this vibrant vacation spot, couples are able to find their own unique opportunities for romantic moments, creating memories that will last a lifetime. Whether it's a quiet evening spent by the water's edge, an exquisite dinner in an elegant setting, or taking an adventure high in the sky on ICON park's 400 ft-high Ferris wheel, Orlando offers a plethora of opportunities for intimate connections.

Join us as we explore the most romantic aspects of Orlando, where love blossoms against the backdrop of a city designed for enchantment. Let the city's charm and allure kindle the sparks of your love story, and together, discover Orlando's hidden gems for extended romantic retreats and date nights alike.

Dinner Dates

Orlando isn't just about exciting dinner theater options and family-friendly dining—it's a place that caters to couples seeking intimate, romantic dinners. These are moments when candlelight sets the stage for enchantment, where every bite and every gaze feel like shared secrets. So, let's take a look at some of the most romantic dining spots Orlando has to offer, where love is on the menu.

Candlelight Charm

In the heart of Orlando, you'll discover a selection of restaurants that have mastered the art of romance. These intimate settings are adorned with soft, flickering candlelight, casting a warm, inviting glow over your evening. The ambiance is designed for lovers to create unforgettable memories. To make it even more special, the chefs prepare exquisite dishes that tantalize the taste buds. From succulent steaks to sushi to tantalizing fresh grilled seafood, you and your partner will embark on a culinary journey through flavors that mirror the passion in your hearts. Here are my recommendations for some of the most romantic restaurants the city has to offer:

Near Disney

- Capa at the Four Seasons
- Bull & Bear
- Victoria and Albert's

Downtown Orlando / Thornton Park / Lake Eola Heights / Colonialtown South

- DoveCote
- The Boheme
- Maxine's on Shine
- Kres
- SOCO
- Jinya

Winter Park

- Garp & Fuss
- Boca

- The Ravenous Pig
- Kedense

Lake Nona

- Chroma
- Bacan

Outside Orlando

- Chef's Table at the Edgewater in Winter Garden
- The Old Jailhouse in Sanford
- Enzo's on the Lake in Longwood

Lake and Riverside Views

Imagine dining by the water's edge as the moon's reflection dances on the surface of the rippling surface. Orlando offers an array of date-night-friendly restaurants that are blessed with lakeside or riverside views. The combination of serene waters, starlit skies, and delectable cuisine creates the perfect recipe for romance. These establishments take dining to the next level, offering not only a feast for the senses but also an opportunity to connect with your loved one on a profound level. Here are my picks for the best dinner destinations with a view of the water:

- Lakeside

- Canvas Restaurant & Market

- Hillstone Restaurant in Winter Park

- St. Johns River Steak & Seafood

Dining in the Clouds

For a dining experience that reaches new heights, consider booking a table for two at one of Orlando's rooftop restaurants. Perched high above the city's bustling streets, these establishments provide an exclusive and intimate atmosphere. With panoramic views of the city, you'll dine amidst the stars and city lights. It's a moment of enchantment where you and your partner can savor each other's company while indulging in fine cuisine. If sky-high dining for your night out sounds good to you, here are my best recommendations:

- BiCE at the at the Loews Portofino Bay Hotel

- Capa at the Four Seasons

- California Grill at Disney's Contemporary Resort

- STK Steakhouse at Disney Springs

Orlando has a remarkable ability to set the scene for romance, and these dining options are the perfect testament to the city's romantic allure. Whether you prefer the flickering candlelight, the soothing waters, or the cityscape views, Orlando has the perfect dinner date spot to suit your romantic preferences.

Couples Activities

Orlando offers couples a whole range of romantic activities to indulge in, making it the ideal destination for those seeking unforgettable moments with their loved ones.

Begin your romantic journey in Orlando with a visit to one of its luxurious spas. These wellness sanctuaries provide a haven for couples to unwind and rejuvenate together. Picture a tranquil atmosphere, soothing aromas, and expert therapists ready to pamper you and your partner. Share the bliss with a couple's massage, a deeply relaxing experience that fosters connection and relaxation.

Whether it's a serene lakeside retreat you're after or an urban spa oasis, Orlando's numerous spas and wellness centers offer an intimate escape from the outside world. The Ritz Carlton spa is known as one of the best, but you need not spend a fortune to be pampered like royalty. Make sure to check websites like Groupon to find the best spa deals during your stay in Orlando; you'll surely find the right spa package for you and your loved one.

Once you've been pampered to your heart's content, take an adventure that soars to new heights; consider taking a tethered hot air balloon ride or jumping on the famous ICON Ferris wheel. If the balloon ride sounds like something right up your alley, Aerophile in Disney Springs is your best bet for experiencing this high-flying magic. They offer an 8-minute tethered ride at a very reasonable price of $25 per person. If you're after a real balloon adventure and are brave enough to go untethered, check out Bob's Balloon Rides in Champion's Gate.

After you've touched back down on the ground, consider a sunset boat ride, such as those found on Lake Eola and Lake Fairview. You can also do a Kayak cruise in Winter Park at Get Up and Go Kayaking, which is found at Dinky Dock. These picturesque voyages are a dream come true for couples who want to revel in the tranquility of the water. Cruising along the lake, you'll witness the fiery hues of a Florida sunset that reflect on the water's surface. As you bask in the serenity, you can savor the company of your partner and the enchanting surroundings.

More Romantic Things to Do

The City Beautiful has a plethora of romantic activities to explore. From charming gardens to elegant wine tastings, there's no shortage of romantic experiences to make your getaway truly special. The options are as diverse as your love story, ensuring that you and your partner create memories that last a lifetime. Here are some more ideas for couples activities:

- Have a movie date night at Silver Moon Drive-In Theater or at the monthly outdoor movie shown at Leu Gardens, which allows BYOB.

- Ride horses at Hidden Palms Ranch in Sanford.

- Catch a Broadway show at the Center for the Performing Arts.

Orlando's romantic side offers couples a wealth of experiences that range from pampering spa days to enchanting sunset boat rides and much more. Whether you're seeking relaxation, adventure, or a little bit of both, Orlando sets the stage for a love story that's uniquely yours.

Where to Stay

Your romantic journey in Orlando deserves the perfect sanctuary, and fortunately, the city is replete with charming and elegant places to stay that cater to couples.

Romantic Hotels

Orlando boasts a selection of charming hotels, perfect for couples seeking a cozy and intimate setting. These accommodations are designed to create an atmosphere of romance, with features like four-poster beds, private balconies, and en-suite Jacuzzis. From historic boutique hotels to secluded resorts, these properties prioritize creating an ambiance that fosters connection.

For couples who want to indulge in opulence, Orlando has an array of luxury accommodations that go above and beyond. These high-end resorts and hotels offer lavish amenities, personalized services, and impeccable attention to detail. From world-class spas and fine dining to private pools and expansive suites, these properties are designed to elevate your romantic getaway to the next level. Whether you're celebrating a special occasion or simply wish to immerse yourselves in luxury, Orlando's upscale lodgings ensure a memorable and indulgent stay, of course, with a steep price tag attached.

Whether you prefer a lakeside view or a lush garden setting, the most romantic hotels in Orlando offer an ideal backdrop for your couple's escape. For the top choices for romantic lodging in Orlando, see the section entitled "Where to Stay" in Chapter 2. The hotels listed under the Luxury Price Range category in that section roughly correspond to the top-rated choices for couples seeking a romantic lodging option. That said, you don't have to spend an arm and a leg to find a nice room with a hot tub in The City Beautiful, so here are some more affordable choices for all you budget-conscious lovebirds out there, all of which have room options for en-suite hot tubs or jacuzzis:

- Grand Villas Resort
- Mariott's Imperial Palms
- Lake Nona Wave Hotel
- Sheraton Vistana
- Buena Vista Suites
- Lowes Portofino Bay
- Grand Bohemian
- Caribe Royale

Cozy Bed and Breakfasts

If you're in search of a more intimate and personalized experience, consider staying at one of the cozy bed and breakfasts outside Orlando and the buzz of the big city. These establishments provide a unique and welcoming environment where you'll be treated to warm hospitality and charming accommodations.

With individually decorated rooms and homemade breakfasts, Central Florida's best B&Bs create a home away from home, ideal for couples looking for a warm and inviting atmosphere. There are a ton of choices of unique, charming places to stay close to Orlando; here are some of my top picks:

- Thurston House in Maitland
- Mount Dora Historic Inn & Cottages in Mount Dora
- Black Dolphin Inn in New Smyrna Beach

- Port D'HIver Bed & Breakfast in Melbourne Beach

The lodging, dining, and activity options found in and around Orlando that are great for couples represent a wide range of options for all different budgets and preferences, from romantic hotels that are centrally located to luxurious resorts and intimate bed and breakfasts. No matter your preferences, the diverse range of options Orlando has to offer ensures that your stay is as memorable and romantic as the moments you'll create together.

Did You Know?

In September 1984, Orlando native Joseph Kittinger II, a United States Air Force officer, took off on an extraordinary solo hot air balloon adventure from Maine all the way to Italy, making his way across the vast expanse of the Atlantic Ocean for more than three days. Joseph sailed through the skies, defying the odds and completing this transatlantic passage with grace and determination, finally touching down in the forests of Montennote in Italy's Liguria region.

So, as you explore the enchanting romantic experiences that Orlando has to offer, remember that the city's history is rich, both with tales of soaring love and boundless adventure—making it the perfect backdrop for creating your own high-flying experiences with your loved one, whether you plan on booking your own in-tethered hot air balloon ride with Bob's Balloons, choose to opt for a short tethered ride with Aerophile, settle on viewing the world from above from the ICON Ferris wheel—or would simply rather engage in activities closer to the ground.

Share Your Insights!

As you dive head-first in love with the romantic escapades Orlando has to offer, we'd love to hear about your own memorable experiences and tips for making the most of your time in the city. Share your special moments, hidden gems you've discovered, and any unique activities you've enjoyed with your partner. By joining the conversation and sharing your insights, you can become part of a vibrant community of fellow travelers seeking to make their Orlando journey unforgettable.

Use the hashtag #DiscoverOrlandoGuide to connect with other readers and adventurers who are exploring the city's romantic side. Your contributions can inspire and assist others in planning their own romantic escapades in Orlando, creating a network of passionate travelers and seekers of love and adventure.

So, don't hesitate to share your experiences and recommendations, and let's make Orlando an even more enchanting and unforgettable destination for all couples seeking the perfect blend of romance and adventure. Your insights can help others embark on their own romantic journey in this vibrant city, so join us in the quest to discover the most romantic hot spots in Orlando!

For All You Solo Travelers Out There: Don't Fret

While Orlando has shown us its enchanting and romantic side, it's essential to remember that the love for adventure and exploration isn't confined to couples alone. For all the solo travelers and those who may not have a romantic partner joining them on their travels, Orlando still holds a world of wonder and excitement.

In this city of endless possibilities, your solo adventure can be just as extraordinary. Embrace the opportunity to connect with your inner explorer, follow your passions, and discover the beauty of self-discovery. Orlando has an abundance of thrilling experiences, remarkable sights, and hidden gems waiting for you to uncover. So, whether you're seeking exhilarating theme park adventures, serene moments of reflection, or a mix of both, Orlando has something extraordinary in store for you.

Remember, the most important person to love and cherish on this journey is yourself. Celebrate your independence, and let Orlando be your canvas for self-discovery, personal growth, and creating unforgettable memories. Your solo adventure can be just as magical and meaningful as any romantic escapade, and Orlando is the perfect backdrop for your unique story.

So, to all you solo travelers and free spirits, Orlando welcomes you with open arms.: Your personal adventure is a celebration of self-love, exploration, and the pure joy of discovery. Embrace it with open hearts and open minds, and let Orlando be the stage for your extraordinary solo travel experience to flourish!

Chapter 8:

Solo Time in Orlando

Are you a solo traveler seeking adventure, culture, and experiences beyond the ordinary? Orlando isn't just a city for families and couples; rather, it presents a whole range of opportunities and activities for those traveling alone. Whether you're an experienced solo backpacker or it's your first time traveling solo, this chapter is dedicated to making your Orlando journey unforgettable.

From dining alone at world-class restaurants to discovering cultural gems and staying safe and happy throughout your trip, we've got you covered. Let's start planning your very own customizable solo Orlando adventure, where the magic is yours to create.

Do It Your Way

Orlando, often associated with family vacations, may not seem like the typical destination for solo travelers. However, the city has a lot to offer to those visiting alone. One of the best advantages of traveling solo in Orlando is the freedom to create a unique and self-paced experience at its renowned theme parks. You're not bound by group dynamics or schedules, allowing you to go at your own speed, explore what interests you the most, and make the most of your visit.

Dining alone in Orlando can be a delightful experience, and the city offers a variety of restaurants where solo diners are not only comfortable but also encouraged. From cozy cafes to upscale eateries, you can savor your meals at your own pace without the need for conversation if you prefer solitude. Whether it's a quiet breakfast, a leisurely lunch, or a candlelit dinner, Orlando's dining scene welcomes solo travelers with open arms. So, don't hesitate to indulge in delicious dishes and embrace the freedom to dine exactly as you wish. Here are some of the best spots to dine solo at:

- Delaney's Tavern
- The Monroe
- Stasios

- The Moderne
- Santiago's Bodega
- Tori Tori
- Jinya Ramen
- DOMU Dr. Phillips
- Rusteak
- Bulla's Gastrobar

While Orlando can be enjoyed alone, meeting new friends along the way can enhance your experience. Whether you're interested in group tours, local meetups, or community events, there are plenty of opportunities to connect with like-minded people during your trip. It's a chance to share your adventure, explore the city together, and maybe even form lasting bonds. So, if you're looking to add a social dimension to your solo adventure, Orlando provides ample options for meeting new friends and enjoying the city's attractions in good company.

But that's not all! Orlando has a whole host of activities that are ideal for solo travelers, from thrilling adventures to cultural explorations. Here are some of the best ones to consider:

- Join a Disney meetup group to mingle with other solo travelers.
- Sign up for a group yoga or fitness activity.
- Go on a bioluminescence kayak tour with BK Adventure to see glowing algae and aquatic life up close.

- Take a cooking class at a local culinary program such as Truffles and Trifles.

- Attend events at museums or art gallery openings.

- Sign up for a guided walking tour of the city, such as the Downtown Orlando Ghost Tour.

Culture Stops

Orlando isn't just about theme parks and world-class entertainment spectacles; it also has a quieter, less flashy side, including a vibrant cultural scene waiting to be explored by solo travelers. If you're a culture enthusiast, you'll find numerous art galleries and museums in the city where you can indulge in a dose of creativity and history. Here are some recommendations for those looking to embrace Orlando's cultural side:

For Art Lovers

Orlando is home to several art museums and galleries that showcase a diverse range of artistic expressions. From contemporary art to historical exhibitions, these cultural institutions offer a deep dive into the creative spirit of the city. Whether you're interested in visual arts, sculpture, or photography, there's an art space for you to explore. Be sure to check out the links provided for more information on specific museums and galleries. Here are some of the best ones to check out during your visit:

- Orlando Museum of Art
- Mennello Museum of American Art
- Charles Hosmer Morse Museum of American Art
- Rollins Museum of Art
- Cornell Fine Arts Museum

- Zore Neale Hurston National Museum of Fine Arts

- Modernism Museum Mount Dora

- Downtown Orlando Arts District

Cultural Festivals

Orlando hosts a variety of off-park cultural festivals throughout the year, celebrating art, music, food, and diverse cultures. These events are not only enjoyable but also an excellent opportunity to connect with fellow travelers and locals who share your interests. Keep an eye on the city's event calendar to see if any cultural festivals align with your visit; small, local events such as these could add a unique and enriching dimension to your solo trip:

- Scottish Highland Games

- Dragon Parade

- Mardi Gras

- Puerto Rican Parade

- Oktoberfest

Historic Buildings

For history buffs or those who appreciate the architectural heritage of a place, Orlando offers a treasure trove of old and historic buildings. From charming colonial-style structures to iconic landmarks, these sites reveal the city's past and are cool to see for their historical significance and architectural beauty.

A visit to these buildings can provide insights into the evolution of Orlando over the years:

- Atlantic Coastline Station
- Old Orlando Railroad Depot
- Harry P. Leu House
- Mizell Cemetery
- Kress Building
- Pappy Kennedy House
- Dr. William Monroe Wells House
- Hendry-Walker House
- Davis Armory
- Judge John Cheney House
- Rogers Building
- S. Howard Atha House
- Wells' Built Hotel
- United States Post Office and Court House

On your solo journey, let yourself be enriched by the rich history, art, and festivities that this city has to offer. With a myriad of options available, you're sure to find experiences that resonate with your cultural interests and leave you with lasting memories.

Stay Safe and Happy

Safety and happiness go hand in hand when traveling solo in Orlando. As a solo traveler, it's crucial to take precautions to ensure a secure and enjoyable journey. Safety should be a top priority for female solo travelers. While it's by no means a dangerous city, make sure to pack your pepper spray and emergency whistle.

Make sure to use reputable transport options when getting around Orlando. Trusted rideshare services and well-established transportation companies can provide you with a secure way to navigate the city. Additionally, make sure to choose accommodations in well-lit and populated areas to enhance your safety.

Budget Tips for Solo Travelers

Traveling solo doesn't have to break the bank. Orlando offers various budget-friendly options that can help you make the most of your trip without draining your wallet. From dining at affordable local eateries to taking advantage of discounts and deals at theme parks and attractions, there are numerous ways to save money without compromising your experience. Here are some tips:

- Make a budget *before* you start booking your itinerary.

- Visit during the off-season.

- Don't dine out for every meal.

- Stay in lodging outside of the parks.

- Look for discounted tickets and passes, but be aware of any restrictions.

- Watch out for tempting add-ons and extra fees at the parks.

The Power of Flexibility

One of the joys of solo travel is the freedom to adapt your plans on the go. Embrace the flexibility that solo travel allows and be open to serendipitous experiences. You might discover hidden gems or meet interesting people when you're not tied to a rigid itinerary. Use the links provided to learn about travel planning and how to set up the perfect itinerary that leaves room for spontaneity.

Remember, solo travel in Orlando can be an incredibly rewarding experience. By prioritizing safety, managing your budget wisely, and staying open to the unexpected, you'll be well-equipped to make the most of your journey and create lasting memories in this vibrant city.

Did You Know?

For solo travelers exploring the diverse attractions of Orlando, it's worth knowing that not far from the city lies Florida's Space Coast, a paradise for surf enthusiasts and beach lovers. Don't worry; we'll let you in an all the secrets of the Space Coasts' beaches in the next chapter: Chapter 9: Day Trips.

Cocoa Beach, in particular, has gained recognition as the surfing capital of Florida's East Coast. This unofficial title isn't just relevant to those who are crazy about catching waves but also to those who are immersed in a unique surf culture that has left a mark on Florida's Atlantic coastline.

The surfing legacy of Cocoa Beach can be attributed to Dick Catri, a surfing legend who made waves in multiple U.S. Championships and represented the United States during the 1967 Duke Kahanamoku Invitational in Hawaii. His contribution to the sport led to his induction into the Surfing Hall of Fame. But it wasn't just his personal achievements that left a lasting impression, as Catri played a pivotal role in showcasing the incredible surfing potential of Florida's coasts.

Cocoa Beach Pier, now known as the Westgate Cocoa Beach Pier, was a hub for surf enthusiasts and hosted numerous competitions. This iconic location attracted local surf legends like Kelly Slater and Todd Holland.

Even if you're not a surfer yourself, a visit to the Westgate Cocoa Beach Pier is a must on your itinerary. It offers not only stunning ocean views but also a chance to soak in the vibrant surf culture that has thrived in this coastal community for decades. So, whether you're a seasoned surfer or simply looking for a relaxing day at the beach, Cocoa Beach and its surfing history are well worth exploring during your Orlando adventure.

Share Your Insights!

Your solo journey through Orlando offers a world of possibilities, and your unique experiences can inspire and guide fellow travelers. Share your insights, discoveries, and adventures on your favorite social media platforms using the hashtag #DiscoverOrlandoGuide. Let your stories, photos, and recommendations become a source of inspiration for others embarking on their solo adventures in this vibrant city.

Whether you've uncovered hidden gems, tried exciting activities, or found fantastic dining spots, your insights can help fellow solo travelers make the most of their Orlando experience. So, don't hesitate to join the conversation and contribute to the collective knowledge of Orlando's diverse offerings. Your solo adventure is a story waiting to be shared, and your insights may be the key to unlocking someone else's memorable journey through the heart of Central Florida!

Think You've Seen It All Yet?

If you think you've seen all of Orlando, think again. While this bustling city offers a plethora of attractions and activities to keep you entertained for days on end, there's a whole world of exploration just beyond its borders. Get ready for some exciting day trips that will take you on a journey to discover new wonders, unique experiences, and hidden treasures in the vicinity of Orlando.

From charming coastal towns to natural wonders and historic landmarks, the surrounding areas of Orlando hold captivating adventures for those willing to venture beyond the city limits. Stay tuned for our next chapter, where we'll guide you through some of the most exciting and unforgettable day trips you can embark on, ensuring your Orlando adventure is filled with surprises and new horizons, whether you're there alone or with the whole family in tow.

Chapter 9:

Day Trips

Are you ready to take a break from the hustle and bustle of Orlando and explore the vast range of wonders that lie just a short drive away? In this chapter, we'll guide you through a variety of day-trip ideas that will add a touch of adventure to your Orlando experience. Whether you're seeking the calming embrace of coastal shores, the natural beauty of Florida's wilderness, or a cultural exploration of nearby towns, we've got you covered.

Each section in this chapter will reveal exciting day-trip destinations and provide you with a glimpse of what each location has to offer. From relaxing on the pristine beaches of Cocoa Beach to snorkeling with gentle manatees in Crystal River, there's something to suit every taste. So, pack your bags, hit the road, and get ready to uncover the wonders that await just beyond Orlando's city limits.

Near the Ocean

Orlando, of course, isn't right on the coast, but within just a short drive, you can find yourself surrounded by the serene beauty of the Atlantic Ocean or even the Florida Gulf if you're up for a bit of a longer drive over to Tampa Bay. In this section, we'll introduce you to a selection of charming coastal destinations that make for perfect day trips from Orlando.

Beaches

- **Cocoa Beach:** Located approximately an hour's drive from Orlando, close to the Kennedy Space Center, Cocoa Beach offers a perfect blend of relaxation and adventure. With its golden sands and rolling waves, it's a haven for beach lovers and surf enthusiasts. If you're in the mood for something more than sunbathing, explore the iconic pier or take a kayak tour through the Indian River Lagoon.

- **New Smyrna Beach:** A bit further North up the coastline, you'll find New Smyrna Beach, known for its laid-back atmosphere and friendly locals. This beach town is ideal for those seeking a quieter escape. Stroll along the historic avenue of the quaint town, or try your hand at fishing.

- **Daytona Beach:** Continuing up the Atlantic coast from New Smyrna, you'll find Daytona Beach, which is famous for its hard-packed sandy shores. Besides enjoying the sun and sea, you can drive your car right onto the beach, a unique experience in itself. Daytona is also home to the Daytona International Speedway, where you can catch a thrilling NASCAR stock car race.

- **Clearwater Beach**: If you're keen to explore Florida's Gulf Coast and are keen to explore Tampa Bay, Clearwater Beach is about two and a half hours from Orlando. Known for its powdery white sands and crystal-clear waters, this beach destination is the perfect place for water sports, dolphin-watching cruises, and picturesque sunsets.

Serene Seaside Towns

Old Town St. Augustine

Now, this is a place where history and a unique blend of Spanish-tinged Floridian charm come together seamlessly. This historic city is about an hour and 45 minutes away from Orlando and boasts a captivating blend of colonial architecture, cobblestone streets, and a rich cultural heritage. Wander through the ancient streets of the Historic District, where you'll find Spanish-inspired architecture, centuries-old forts, and quaint shops. Be sure to visit the Castillo de San Marcos, the oldest masonry fort in the continental United States, and experience a taste of history in a picturesque setting.

As you venture through the historical streets of St. Augustine, you'll discover why this city is often referred to as the "Ancient City." It's a day trip that will transport you back in time while providing modern-day delights, making it a perfect escape from the bustling Orlando scene.

Nature-Oriented Day Trips

Just a scenic car ride away from Orlando lies a world of natural wonders waiting to be explored. In this section, we'll take you on a tour of some of the most stunning natural day trip destinations throughout the Sunshine State that are easily accessible from Orlando, giving you a bunch of further-flung options that aren't included in Chapter 4: Nature Time in Orlando.

Blue Springs

A short drive from Orlando, Blue Springs State Park is an oasis of crystal-clear water and lush foliage. The main attraction here is the cool, spring-fed waters that remain at a constant 72 °F year-round. While swimming in the two concrete-ringed pools is a popular activity, what truly sets Blue Springs apart is the chance to witness Florida's manatees in their natural environment! But you don't have to jump into to the underground spring-fed pools to have a good time here. There's an observation boardwalk where you can stroll along as you spot local wildlife.

During the winter months, manatees seek refuge in the warmer waters of Blue Springs, making it an ideal time for visitors to spot these gentle giants as they come further inland from the cooling waters of the Atlantic Ocean. Blue Springs is truly one of the best places right near Orlando, where you can immerse yourself in the beauty of Florida's natural world while connecting with its unique wildlife.

Crystal River

If you're a dedicated manatee enthusiast after checking out Blue Springs, Crystal River should be the next manatee-spotting haven on your day trip radar. Located just a couple of hours from Orlando on the Gulf Coast—this scenic spot is renowned for one extraordinary wildlife encounter: Swimming with manatees!

Crystal River is one of the few places in the world where you can get up close and personal with these gentle giants in their natural habitat. Unlike Blue Springs, where you're more likely to spot these majestic creatures only during the winter months, the manatees over at Crystal River are more likely to hang out year-round. That said, their presence and numbers can fluctuate seasonally, and your best bet is always to visit between November and April when they seek the warmer waters of the springs.

The Crystal River National Wildlife Refuge provides a safe haven for these endangered creatures, which inhabit the spring-red river, and the guided tours they offer take you on an unforgettable adventure. Don't forget your snorkeling gear! That's right! You're able to slip under the crystal-clear waters and catch a great view of these remarkable, gentle marine mammals.

Ocala National Forest

For those seeking outdoor adventures, Ocala National Forest, approximately an hour and a half from Orlando, is a wilderness playground. With its lush pine forests, pristine lakes, and clear springs, it's known as a haven for hikers, campers, and water enthusiasts. You can look forward to exploring the Ocala section of the Florida Trail, a network of scenic trails that wind through the forest.

You can even pitch your tent or park your RV in one of the many campgrounds and RV parks. Dispersed camping is allowed in the park, and there are also two Civilian Conservation Corps cabins that can be reserved through the U.S. Forest Service. If roughing it out in the wilderness without running water and bathrooms is not your forte, there are glamping options too, with private cabins with electricity, showers, TV, and all the amenities and creature comforts you'd expect!

Before We Move On

These natural day trips near Orlando offer a breath of fresh air and a chance to connect with the great outdoors. Whether you're snorkeling with manatees, hiking through a national forest, or swimming in a pristine spring, you're sure to create lasting memories in these natural wonders, just a short drive away from the city. Now it's time to get some culture!

Cultural Day Trips

For the culture aficionados and history buffs, Orlando serves as a gateway to a wide variety of enriching day trip destinations. Let's explore some of these cultural gems that are just a stone's throw away from The City Beautiful.

The Villages

Located to the northwest of Orlando, The Villages is a planned community that offers a unique cultural experience. Known for its active and lively atmosphere, The Villages is a haven for retirees and visitors alike. So hop in a golf cart, or get your walking cane out, and get with the local vibe!

In The Villages, visitors are welcome to take leisurely strolls through the picturesque Spanish Springs Town Square, play a round of golf at one of the world-class country clubs found there, enjoy live entertainment at the 1,000-seat Sharon L. Morse Performing Arts Center, and savor a wide array of dining options. The charming atmosphere and vibrant arts scene make this a perfect day trip destination for those looking to immerse themselves in a distinctive Florida community.

St. Cloud

Positioned on the southern shore of East Lake Tohopekaliga, St. Cloud offers visitors a vibrant cultural and historical experience along the banks of the lake's calm, crystal-clear waters. Start with one of the city's walking tours to uncover its historical charm. Then, pop over to the St. Cloud Heritage Museum, which showcases the city's history through exhibits and artifacts.

Originally started as a community for veterans of the Civil War, with its quaint streets and serene lake views, St. Cloud is certainly a peaceful retreat where you can connect with Florida's past with some authentic Americana. If you're a fan of snakes and other reptiles, you'll also want to check out Reptile World Serpentarium, a small, local zoo with over 80 species of reptiles, including crocs, gators, and lizards of various types.

Mount Dora

A short drive northwest of Orlando, Mount Dora is a delightful town with a charming historic district. There, you can stroll down the tree-lined streets and explore a variety of unique boutiques and galleries. A visit to the Mount Dora History Museum is recommended. There, you can learn about the town's rich past.

A scenic boat tour on Lake Dora will put you in the mood for more exploration. Known for its annual art festivals, antique shops, and welcoming atmosphere, Mount Dora offers a cultural escape with a touch of artistic flair.

Before We Move On

These cultural day trips from Orlando are exemplary in highlighting the diversity of experiences you can encounter in Central Florida. Whether you prefer the lively ambiance of The Villages, the historical allure of St. Cloud, or the artistic charm of Mount Dora, each destination promises an enriching and culturally immersive adventure that teaches visitors about what makes the tiny towns of Florida tick.

Did You Know?

While Orlando may be known for its theme parks and attractions, there are hidden gems along Florida's Atlantic coastline waiting to be discovered. Melbourne Beach, located approximately 80 miles from Orlando on the Space Coast, is one such treasure. What makes Melbourne Beach unique is not just its pristine shores but also its rich history.

The town is Brevard County's oldest beach community, with a history dating back to the 1500s when the famous explorer

Juan Ponce de León first set foot on the shores of what they called at that time" La Florida." Although it wasn't officially incorporated as a town until 1883, its historical significance is undeniable.

Today, Melbourne Beach offers a serene escape from the hustle and bustle of more touristy beaches. Its expansive coastline provides ample space for relaxation, making it an ideal destination for families with young children who seek a quieter and less crowded beach where they can play and unwind. Melbourne Beach's historical roots and tranquil beauty make it a wonderful day trip destination from Orlando, allowing you to explore Florida's past while enjoying the peaceful present.

Share Your Insights!

As we've explored Orlando's diverse offerings and ventured on delightful day trips, we'd love to hear from you, our fellow adventurers. Your experiences, tips, and discoveries can be a source of inspiration for others looking to embark on their own day trips from Orlando and other locations around Central Florida. Share your insights, recommendations, and travel tales with us, and don't forget to use our dedicated hashtag: #DiscoverOrlandoGuide.

Whether you've uncovered hidden gems, enjoyed unique activities, or have valuable insights to offer, your contributions can enhance the Orlando experience for fellow travelers. So, go ahead and share your Orlando adventures, and let's build a vibrant community of explorers and adventurers together!

I've Got a Secret For You

Now that we've seen all the most thrilling day trips around Central Florida let's uncover some of Orlando's best-kept secrets. In our final chapter, Chapter 10: Insiders Guide, you'll get tips on how locals get around The City Beautiful, how they have fun, and how they kick back all while enjoying the Florida Sun. In this chapter, we'll give you exclusive access to some of the best lesser-known spots and tips for a unique travel experience.

Chapter 10:

An Insider's Guide

Welcome to the final chapter of our Orlando adventure: Insider's Guide. If you've ever wanted to uncover the lesser-known gems of this vibrant city, you're in for a treat. As we've seen so far, Orlando is more than just theme parks and tourist attractions—it's a destination full of hidden spots, local favorites, and vacation pro tips that can elevate your experience from ordinary to extraordinary.

So, slap on that sunscreen and get ready to navigate Orlando like a local, armed with insider knowledge that'll help you unlock the city's best-kept secrets and have the best vacation ever. Let's dive into the heart of Orlando's unique features that lie just off the beaten path and discover what makes this city truly special for locals and visitors alike.

Odd and Fun Spots

Unlocking Orlando's hidden gems goes beyond the ordinary. In this section, we'll take a look at a few quirky attractions to add to your list of activities you can only find in Orlando.

Butterfly Encounter at Harry P. Leu Gardens

We already mentioned a bunch of happenings at this happening manse, including the film series where you can bring your own picnic (and even booze), but did you know you can also immerse yourself in a magical world of fluttering wings there?

The Butterfly Encounter, housed within the Leu Gardens, invites you to wander through a habitat filled with colorful butterflies, providing an enchanting experience for insect enthusiasts and admirers of beauty! You might even spot a few fairies or sprites as you cavort around these enchanting grounds.

If you were wondering whether they have a gift shop, of course they do! There, you can find gardening equipment to start your own enchanted garden, as well as some conveniently placed vending machines for refreshments.

Randall Knife Museum

Nestled in the heart of Orlando, the Randall Knife Museum is a unique museum for knife enthusiasts that features over 7,000 examples of razor-sharp implements for cutting, maiming, or just whipping up some delicious grub. The remarkable collection includes a wide range of handmade knives, axes, swords, and other sharp tools of utility and warfare, each crafted with expert precision. The museum offers visitors a fascinating tour through the artistry and craftsmanship of these exceptional hand-ground and honed blades.

In a nod to nearby Cape Canaveral and Kennedy Space Center, their collection even features the first knife that ever went to space aboard Gordon Cooper's 1963 orbital mission. What he planned to use it for up there remains a mystery to both you and me, but nonetheless, here, you'll find it in all its glory!

The museum is part of the Randall Knives factory and store, and as you'd imagine, the outlet store is filled with razor-sharp hunting and kitchen cutlery, all handcrafted and honed to perfection.

Jack Kerouac House

Literature lovers and beatnik enthusiasts won't want to miss the chance to visit the former home of renowned author Jack Kerouac. This unassuming house in the College Park neighborhood served as Kerouac's residence, where he penned the iconic novel "On the Road." The house is now a literary landmark offering insights into the life of this influential writer.

A tour of the historical house where one of the most pivotal works of 20th-century American literature was penned offers a glimpse into the environment that fueled the creation of this literary masterpiece. The preserved artifacts and exhibits within the house serve as a time capsule, allowing visitors to connect with the spirit of the Beat Generation and gain a deeper understanding of Kerouac's motivations and artistic vision.

Global Convergence Sculpture

Immerse yourself in the intersection of art and technology with the Global Convergence Sculpture, a puzzling work of art by Alabama-based sculptor DeeDee Morrison. Located at the Orlando International Airport, this captivating artwork combines elements of nature and optical illusions with what appears to be real live bass swimming around inside! Wait, but on second look, you'll realize that the fish are, in fact, just printed on transparent layers of blue plastic.

The secret behind how the artist got these fish to look so realistic can be traced back to ancient Japan, where artworks used ink-stamped prints of real fish in a process called *Gyotakyu*. This ancient fish-print technique, combined with clever usage of lighting techniques, causes the fish to glow with life-like authenticity.

And the meaning of the piece? You might ask yourself. Well, It's supposed to symbolize the diverse global connections made possible through travel, something you're well aware of by now as a seasoned travel enthusiast yourself!

Disney Progress City Model

Did you know that you can explore the past of Disney's innovative vision without traveling back in time? At the Walt Disney World Resort, you'll find The Progress City Model, originally designed by Walt Disney himself, provides a glimpse into the experimental prototype "community of tomorrow" he originally envisioned.

This detailed scale model showcases the visionary Space Age ideas that ultimately shaped the theme parks we know today, giving us insight into the creative process behind the park's creation and what was imagined it could one day become. While this futuristic diorama never materialized into a real-life city, it stands as a shining example of the power of dreams and the enduring impact of Walt Disney's pioneering spirit.

Disney's vision of the future shows us that even when faced with the complexities of the present, there's immense value in revisiting the visions of the past to inform and bring inspiration to the possibilities and pursuits of tomorrow.

Disney Collection at Orange County Regional History Center

Unearth the magic and history behind Disney's legacy at the Orange County Regional History Center, which is housed in a beautiful courthouse building in Downtown Orlando that was built in 1927. The Disney Collection features a captivating array of artifacts and memorabilia, chronicling the evolution of the beloved theme parks and the old Walt himself, the creative genius behind it all.

Aside from the Disney Collection, you'll find three entire floors of permanent exhibit spaces filled with historical artifacts and treasures from all over the Sunshine State, some dating back as long as 12,000 years (*16 Cool and Unusual Things to Do in Orlando*, 2023).

Before We Move On

As you make your way through Orlando's odd attractions, you'll discover a city that thrives on the extraordinary and beckons you to explore the unexpected.

Local Favorites

Orlando isn't just a destination for tourists; it's a thriving city with a wealth of offerings for locals and visitors alike. Act like and mingle with locals by checking out these insider favorites.

Farmer's Markets

For a true taste of Orlando's local flavor, explore the vibrant fresh markets scattered throughout the city and in surrounding towns and cities, all of which feature a wide range of locally sourced products. From seasonal produce to handcrafted goods, these markets offer a delightful sensory experience. Here are the ones to check out if you want to get the local experience:

lo Farmer's Market at Lake Eola Park

- Winter Park Farmer's Market
- Winter Garden Farmer's Market
- East Orlando Farmer's Market

Near Orlando

- Celebration Farmer's Market in Kissimmee
- Windermere Farmer's Market at Windermere Town Square
- Oviedo Farmers Market in Oviedo
- Downtown Mount Dora Farmer's Market in Mount Dora
- Longwood Farmer's Market in Longwood
- Lake Nona Farmers Market in Lake Nona Center
- Sanford Farmer's Market in Sanford
- Clermont Farmer's Market in Downtown Clermont
- Maitland Farmer's Market in Maitland
- Auduban Park Community Market

- Lake Mary's Farmer's Market in Lake Mary

Orlando's Craft Breweries

The craft beer scene demonstrates Orlando's dynamic and evolving culture. Indulge in a wide variety of craft beers at some of the most popular breweries and bars. Whether you're a seasoned craft beer enthusiast or a newcomer to the scene, Orlando's local brews are sure to leave a lasting impression. Here are the best places to sit down for a frosty mug:

Near the Parks

- Half Barrel Beer Project

Near Downtown

- Big Storm Brewing Company Orlando Taproom at the Amway Center

- Broken Strings Brewery in Parramore

- Deadwords Brewing in Callahan

- Sideward Brewing in the Milk District

- Ivanhoe Park Brewing Company in Park Lake / Highland

- Ten10 Brewing Company in Park Lake / Highland

Audubon Park

- Redlight, Redlight

Baldwin Park

- Tactical Brewing Company

Lake Holden

- Rockpit Brewing

Fort Gatlin

- Gatlin Hall Brewing in Forth Gatlin

At Orlando International

- Cask & Larder at Orlando International Airport

Smooth Trip Tips

Navigating Orlando like a local involves more than just visiting the popular spots. All you have to do to blend in with the locals is embrace the city's rhythm and flow. There are a few ways you gain insights into how people live down here that enhance your overall experience. Here, I'll explain.

Local Transportation Know-How

Local knowledge is your secret weapon for a hassle-free trip. One of the best ways to get around Orlando if you don't have a rental car is by utilizing ride-sharing apps like Uber or Lyft. Here's how else you can get around with ease:

- **public transportation:** Orlando boasts a well-connected public transportation system, including an extensive network of buses and the SunRail commuter train. Consider using these eco-friendly, cost-effective options to navigate the city and its surrounding areas.

- **biking:** Orlando has become increasingly bike-friendly in recent years, with numerous dedicated bike lanes and trails. Many neighborhoods and attractions provide bike rentals, offering a scenic and active way to explore the city.

- **walking:** Certain areas of Orlando are pedestrian-friendly. Take a leisurely stroll to discover local shops, cafes, and hidden gems in neighborhoods such as Thornton Park and Baldwin Park.

Blend In With the Locals

To truly immerse yourself in Orlando's culture, learn the art of talking and acting like a local. Connect with residents, strike up conversations, and embrace the city's vibrant atmosphere. Discover the nuances of Florida's unique language and social cues, enhancing your interactions and unlocking authentic experiences.

Did you know that there's actually a new dialect of the English language emerging in South Florida right now as we speak? When you travel to Miami, for instance, instead of saying, "Get out of the car," say, "Get down from the car." *Why?* You might ask? Well, linguists have noticed this change in the influence of

Spanish speakers on English, even among Floridian populations that have no knowledge of Spanish at all. So, if you remember this nifty trick and use it in conversation, Orlando locals may even think you're a Floridian yourself.

Packing Wisdom for Orlando

Orlando's weather and variety of indoor and outdoor activities demand thoughtful packing. Bringing clothing that's suitable for the Florida climate is a must, and you wouldn't want to forget essentials for theme park adventures. Here are a few more packing tips:

- **sun protection:** With the Florida sun shining brightly, sunscreen, sunglasses, and a wide-brimmed hat are useful in protecting yourself from harmful UV rays. Stay sun-safe, especially during outdoor activities.

- **comfortable footwear:** Expect lots of walking, especially if you plan on exploring the theme parks. Bring comfortable, supportive sneakers to keep your feet happy throughout your adventures.

- **rain gear:** Orlando is known for its sudden rain showers, even on sunny days. Pack a lightweight, compact umbrella or a poncho to stay dry during brief rain spells.

- **water:** Staying hydrated is crucial, especially in the Florida heat. Carry a reusable water bottle to refill throughout the day and stay refreshed.

- **light layers:** While the days can be warm, winter evenings in Orlando can bring a slight chill. Pack light layers to accommodate changing temperatures, ensuring you're comfortable day and night.

- **theme park essentials:** When heading out to visit the theme parks, consider bringing a small backpack to carry essentials like snacks, a refillable water bottle, and a portable battery to charge your devices with.

- **bug spray:** If you plan to explore natural areas or attend outdoor events, having a DEET-containing bug spray can make your experience more enjoyable, particularly during the more hot and humid months of summer, when mosquitos are biting the most.

Did You Know?

Orlando boasts a historic treasure that whispers tales of the past. Church Street Station, also known as the Old Orlando Railroad Depot, demonstrates the city's rich history and harkens back to the age when trains to Florida were a novel concept.

Constructed in 1889, this distinguished train station served as a busy rail transport and freight hub until 1926, connecting communities and facilitating the movement of people and goods. Today, the station is honored with a place on the National Register of Historic Places, acknowledging its significance in shaping Orlando's narrative.

Orlando's modern-day commuter rail system, Sun Rail, has a station near the old one, where countless commuters weave their way through the same space that once echoed with the rhythms of departing and arriving trains, carrying the values and aspirations of a bygone era.

As you explore Orlando, take a moment to wander through Church Street Station. Feel the echoes of history reverberate through its walls, connecting the past with the present. It's a chance to step back in time, appreciating the layers of stories that have shaped Orlando into the vibrant city it is today.

Share Your Insights!

Your Orlando trip will surely be filled with unforgettable experiences, discoveries, and hidden gems. That's why I'd like to invite you to share your insights, tips, and favorite moments from all around the City Beautiful. Whether you stumbled upon a charming local spot, uncovered a lesser-known attraction, or have a must-try recommendation, your perspective enriches the collective exploration.

Connect with fellow travelers and contribute to the vibrant community of Orlando enthusiasts. Share your stories on social media using #DiscoverOrlandoGuide. Your insights may just be the key to unlocking someone else's unforgettable Orlando journey. Join us in shaping the ultimate guide to the heart of Florida's magic!

Bidding Farewell to "The City Beautiful"

From the towering attractions to the quaint local haunts, we've explored the diverse facets of Orlando's charm, and you've now learned to live like a local, too!

Remember the thrills, the flavors, and the moments that created your personal Orlando travel experience. Whether you discovered a secluded park, indulged in local flavors, or simply enjoyed the rhythm of this city, your adventure has left an indelible mark.

As you bid farewell to "The City Beautiful," carry the memories, the insider tips, and the warmth of Orlando's welcome with you. May your future travels be as captivating as the tales spun within the heart of Florida's magic. Until we meet again, happy trails and safe travels!

Bonus Chapter:

Off the Beaten Path

Orlando's Hidden Flavors

Venture off the beaten path to discover hidden, strange, and thrilling flavors that exist on the periphery of the local food scene we explored in previous chapters. Don't be afraid to explore neighborhoods, even further-flung ones, to find your own hidden gems, from authentic ethnic eateries to innovative fusion cuisine.

Indulge in Central Florida's best-kept culinary secrets, some of which might seem off-putting at first. These authentic places are where passionate under-the-radar chefs create dishes that reflect the true essence of Florida. Here are some of the best spots to taste Orlando's secret flavors:

Fried Gator and Frog

If fried alligator tails and frog legs sound like something you might want to try, head over to Lone Cabbage Fish Camp on St. Johns River. This airboat tour operator that doubles as a fried food stand is a great place to try some of the most authentic flavors of Florida.

Asian Markets Galore

If taking a tour of local wet markets, where the exotic are the East come both within arm's reach and within nose whiff—you have to get down to either Tien Hung Market or Saigon Market, both found in Orlando's Little Saigon area between Colonialtown and Park Lake / Highland. Whether you're looking for some illicit durian fruit or have a craving for squid jerky, you're bound to find some interesting flavors at these hotspots for the brave of palate.

Speakeasies and Dives

From hidden entranceways to unmarked doors to places that look a bit run-down but are actually great—these establishments offer a glimpse into Orlando's vibrant and eclectic nightlife.

Speakeasies

Hanson's Shoe Repair

As you might know, this place is not a cobbler's shop, as its sign might suggest, but rather a high-end cocktail bar. You can find it in Downtown Orlando. Just make sure you know the password to get in!

Mathers Social Gathering

ated in Downtown Orlando's Phoenix building, this secret spot is hidden behind a bookshelf inside an unassuming vintage furniture showroom. The cush cocktail bar you'll find inside isn't cheap, so it might not be the best place to stay all night if you're looking for a budget-friendly tipple.

Dive Bars

Wally's Bar and Liquors in Colonialtown

This eccentric dive bar with a vintage neon sign and a classic jukebox is a great place to go and meet some interesting locals. Yes, it's a liquor store and also a bar to boot!

Nora's Sugar Shack

This dog-friendly hangout might look like it's someone's house, but its hand-lettered facade will clue you into the fact that there's beer, wine, and cigars for sale inside this ramshackle shack located in Park Lake / Highland.

Hideaway Bar

This Park Lake / Highland haunt offers cheap drinks and an extensive menu, including wings, burgers, and all types of standard bar fare that's easy on the wallet and the stomach.

Spooky Fun in The City Beautiful

For those intrigued by the supernatural, you may choose to venture into the most haunted places in the City Beautiful, where tales of ghosts and legends come to life. Here are my best recommendations for seeing the spookier side of Orlando:

Haunted Restaurants

- Hamburger Mary's in Downtown Orlando
- Cocktails & Screams in Downtown Orlando

Haunted Rides and Attractions

- Twilight Zone Tower of Terror at Hollywood Studios in Disney World
- The Haunted Mansion at Magic Kingdom in Disney World

Ghost Tours

- Orlando Haunts, operated by US Ghost Adventures
- HR Interactive Ghost Walking Tour

Share Your Insights!

Have you uncovered a hidden gem of your own in Orlando that deserves a spot in the spotlight? Share your off-the-beaten-path discoveries, secret club experiences, or encounters with the oldest and strangest places using the hashtag

#DiscoverOrlandoGuide. Your insights could inspire fellow adventurers and add a unique twist to their Orlando journey. Let's continue to build an engaged community of explorers sharing all the greatest things Orlando has to offer!

Conclusion

Throughout the pages of this guide, we've had a whirlwind journey through the heart of Florida, exploring the magic that makes Orlando a vast repository of experiences beyond its famed beaches, sunny weather, and thrilling theme parks. As we draw the curtain on our adventure, it's time to step back and look at the beautiful vacation dreams we've built. *Ahhhh, a masterpiece!* we say to ourselves. It's time to give yourself a big pat on your back for finally going ahead with booking the Orlando vacation of your dreams.

Beyond the glittering facades of theme parks and tourist hotspots, Orlando is all about discovering magic in unexpected corners. It's a city that beckons exploration, where the rhythm of local life meets the vibrant attractions and spectacles. The essence of this city's allure lies not only in its grand symphonies but also in the nuanced notes of its neighborhoods, local flavors, and cultural enclaves.

Picture yourself strolling through the ritzy enclave of Winter Park, savoring artisanal delights at a local farmer's market, or discovering the hidden gems of Church Street Station. Boasting rights in Orlando isn't measured by the miles walked or the lengths of lines waited in at theme parks but by the moments etched in the heart—the unexpected, the charming, the authentic, quotidian experience of life here.

So, it's well past time to get those bags packed, embrace the unexpected, and set out on an unforgettable journey that'll make you fall in love with the Sunshine State's crown jewel.

In bidding farewell to you, dear reader, remember that its magic is an ever-unfolding story. Just as the city comes to life with each grapefruit-colored sunrise over palm trees that gently sway, your Orlando tale is one that can continue to evolve into a unique personal tale, with every step taken and every memory made.

Before we part, I have one humble request to ask of you: If this guide has proved useful to you and has been able to guide you through the layers of Orlando's enchantment, consider leaving a review. As with the #DiscoverOrlandoGuide hashtag, I've encouraged you to use your positive reviews on this book to help out future adventurers, ensuring they discover the city's magic with the same wonder and joy.

As we close the planning chapter of our great Orlando escape, may your future travels to Central Florida and elsewhere in the world be filled with the spirit of discovery, the promise of the unexpected, and the savvy traveler magic that allows seasoned tourists to turn every trip into a timeless tale. Safe travels, and may your adventures be as wide and open as the sunny skies across the beautiful state of Florida.

Author Biography

About The Author

Throughout my adult life, I've had many experiences in different positions ranging from musician, to shipyard electrician, to industrial millwright electrician, to the owner of a limousine company, to the owner of a real estate investment company, to a licensed commercial instrument pilot and now to a published author.

Given my range of experiences, people kept telling me: "You should write a book, because you have a lot of good ideas." Finally, I decided to take them up on their advice. As I wrote, my stories came to life. My main purpose as an author became clear: That whoever reads my stories, they would receive more value than they expected.

So, it's my pleasure and privilege to create entertaining, educational, and informative stories for you!

R. T. Kagels

References

Adams, H. (2023, October 2). *4 tips to save money on your next Orlando vacation.* WDW Magazine. https://www.wdw-magazine.com/save-money-on-orlando-vacation/

Airboat Tours. (n.d.-a). Boggy Creek Airboat Adventures. https://bcairboats.com/

Airboat Tours. (n.d.-b). Spirit of the Swamp. https://spiritoftheswamp.com/

Alesha, & Jarryd. (2023, August 1). *14 best day trips from Orlando, Florida (2023 guide).* Nomadasaurus. https://www.nomadasaurus.com/day-trips-from-orlando/#10_Blue_Spring_State_Park

Alvin, C. (2023, August 25). *Kayaking in Central Florida under $50 for two.* Orlando Date Night Guide. https://www.orlandodatenightguide.com/2023/08/kayaking-in-orlando/

Ambrose. (2022, August 3). *10 best rooftop restaurants in Orlando, Florida.* Trip101. https://trip101.com/article/rooftop-restaurants-in-orlando

Animal encounters in Orlando. (n.d.). Orlando Insider Vacations. Retrieved October 22, 2023, from https://orlandoinsidervacations.com/animal-encounters-in-orlando/

Annual events in Orlando & Kissimmee - your guide to major festivals. (2023, January 5). Orlando Insider Vacations. https://orlandoinsidervacations.com/annual-events-in-orlando-kissimmee/

Aquatica Orlando | tips & guide to seaworld's water park. (n.d.). Visit Orlando. https://www.visitorlando.com/things-to-do/theme-parks/seaworld-orlando/aquatica-orlando/

Aquatica Orlando FAQ - plan your water park visit | Aquatica Orlando. (n.d.). Aquatica.com. https://aquatica.com/orlando/faq/

Aquatica Orlando: Complete guide and overview. (n.d.). Orlando Informer. https://orlandoinformer.com/seaworld/aquatica-orlando-complete-guide-and-overview/

Average weather in Orlando, Florida, United States, year round - weather spark. (2019). Weather Spark. https://weatherspark.com/y/17721/Average-Weather-in-Orlando-Florida-United-States-Year-Round

Bell, B. (2023, June 19). *20 Orlando bites on a budget.* Visit Orlando. https://www.visitorlando.com/blog/post/orlando-budget-bites/

Best family things to do in Orlando. (n.d.). Hotels.com Phillipenes. https://ph.hotels.com/go/usa/best-family-things-to-do-orlando

The best Orlando ghost tours. (n.d.). Tripadvisor. https://www.tripadvisor.com/Attractions-g34515-Activities-c42-t226-Orlando_Florida.html

The best Orlando transportation. (n.d.). Tripadvisor. https://www.tripadvisor.com.ph/Attractions-g34515-Activities-c59-Orlando_Florida.html

Best times to visit Orlando. (n.d.). U.S. News and World Report. https://travel.usnews.com/Orlando_FL/When_To_Visit/

Blazquez, A., & Nuñez, G. (2023, September 19). *Best Cuban restaurants in Orlando area, from Cubans' perspective.* WKMG. https://www.clickorlando.com/food/2023/09/19/best-cuban-restaurants-in-orlando-area-from-cubans-perspective/

Bordelon, A. (2021, October 13). *Our top ten tips for visiting SeaWorld Orlando.* Orlando Informer. https://orlandoinformer.com/blog/our-top-ten-tips-for-visiting-seaworld-orlando/

Bradley, C. (2023, January 11). *Why visiting SEA LIFE Orlando is a must with kids! Tips and info.* Flying with a Baby - Family Travel. https://www.flyingwithababy.com/why-visiting-sea-life-orlando-is-a-must-with-kids-tips-and-info/

Bricker, T. (2018, January 28). *Tips for taking kids to Disney World.* Disney Tourist Blog. https://www.disneytouristblog.com/disney-world-kids-tips/

Bricker, T. (2022a, January 1). *2022 Universal Orlando planning guide.* Disney Tourist Blog. https://www.disneytouristblog.com/universal-orlando-trip-planning-guide/

Bricker, T. (2022b, July 5). *2022 Epcot food & wine festival guide.* Disney Tourist Blog.

https://www.disneytouristblog.com/epcot-food-wine-festival-guide-tips/

Bricker, T. (2023, July 24). *Disney World planning guide for 2023-2024.* Disney Tourist Blog. https://www.disneytouristblog.com/disney-world-trip-planning-guide/

Britt on the Move. (2022, May 26). *Gatorland Florida.* Brit on the Move. https://britonthemove.com/gatorland-florida/

Canoe and kayak tours. (n.d.). Get Your Guide. https://www.getyourguide.com/orlando-l191/canoe-kayak-tours-tc61/

Caraher, L. (2023, October 19). *Ultimate beginners guide to Orlando theme parks.* Family Travel and Theme Parks. https://fivefortheroad.com/orlando-theme-parks-guide-for-beginners/

Caramanna, C. (2023, June 17). *Affordable Disney World restaurants that don't skimp on the magic.* Chron. https://www.chron.com/life/travel/article/disney-world-restaurants-18119237.php

Central Florida backyard bird identification. (n.d.). Catandturtle. https://www.blog.catandturtle.net/backyard-bird-identification/

Central Florida events and festivals | gotta go Orlando going out guide. (2023). Www.gottagoorlando.com. https://www.gottagoorlando.com/orlando-festivals-and-events

Chapman, D. (2022a, February 23). *Fun spot America guide - Florida's best kept secret.* Park Savers. https://www.parksavers.com/fun-spot-america-florida-guide-tips/

176

Chapman, D. (2022b, June 19). *Ultimate guide to Gatorland, Orlando's kitschiest attraction.* Park Savers. https://www.parksavers.com/ultimate-guide-to-gatorland-orlandos/

Charlton-Moore, K. (2021, July 28). *7 ways to experience Orlando like a local.* Authentic Florida. https://authenticflorida.com/things-to-do-in-orlando/

Cheese, N. (2016, December 16). *When is the best time to visit Orlando?* Top Villas. https://www.thetopvillas.com/blog/florida/best-time-visit-orlando/

Chieffi, T. (2022, December 29). *Everything you need to know about Aquatica Orlando, one of Florida's best family water parks.*

City district main street. (n.d.). Downtown Orlando. https://www.downtownorlando.com/Life/Districts-Neighborhoods/City-District-Main-Street

City of Orlando. (n.d.). Yelp. https://www.yelp.com/biz/city-of-orlando-orlando

CityPASS. (2023, August 11). *5 places to try the best Cuban food in Orlando, Florida.* Citypass. https://www.citypass.com/articles/orlando/taste-the-best-cuban-food-in-orlando-5-must-visit-spots

Craft beer in Orlando: The hoppiest place on Earth. (n.d.). Flywith.virginatlantic.com. https://flywith.virginatlantic.com/eu/en/stories/craft-beer-in-orlando.html

D'Souza, T. (2022, August 18). *The outside guide to Everglades National Park.* Outside Online. https://www.outsideonline.com/adventure-travel/national-parks/everglades-national-park-travel-guide/

Datko, A. (2022, November 22). *I live in Orlando and when I have visitors, these are the 10 places where I recommend they stay — and only one is a Disney hotel.* Insider. https://www.insider.com/where-to-stay-in-orlando-florida-best-hotels

Davis, J. (2023, January 5). *Best time to visit Orlando for weather, prices, and crowds.* Destguides. https://www.destguides.com/united-states/florida/orlando/best-time-to-visit-orlando

Devault, N. (2016, November 14). *6 Orlando area bed & breakfast staycations.* Orlando Date Night Guide. https://www.orlandodatenightguide.com/2016/11/6-orlando-bed-breakfast-staycations/

Dining. (2023). Walt Disney World. https://disneyworld.disney.go.com/en_CA/dining/

Dining alone in Orlando, FL. (2023). Yelp. https://www.yelp.com/search?find_desc=Dining+Alone&find_loc=Orlando%2C+FL

Dinner shows in Orlando & Kissimmee. (2023, June 24). Orlando Insider Vacations. https://orlandoinsidervacations.com/dinner-shows-in-orlando-kissimmee/

Dinner theaters in Orlando. (n.d.). Tripadvisor. https://www.tripadvisor.com/Attractions-g34515-Activities-c58-t117-Orlando_Florida.html

Discover the fascinating history of Orlando. (n.d.). World Travel Guide. https://www.worldtravelguide.net/guides/north-america/united-states-of-america/florida/orlando/history/

Districts + Neighborhoods. (n.d.). Downtown Orlando. https://www.downtownorlando.com/Life/Districts-Neighborhoods

Downtown Orlando Neighborhoods. (2014, February 7). URBANISTA. https://urbanistaorlando.com/downtown-orlando-neighborhoods/

Dymphe. (2021, July 3). *41 things to do alone in Orlando: Solo travel in Orlando.* Dymabroad. https://dymabroad.com/things-to-do-alone-in-orlando/

Dymphe. (2022, February 11). *101 date ideas in Orlando: Romantic things to do in Orlando.* Dymabroad. https://dymabroad.com/date-ideas-in-orlando/

E. Parker, B. (2020, July 6). *Orlando area day trip to Mount Dora, Florida.* Britt with Intent. https://brittwithintent.com/mount-dora-fl-day-trip/

Eagan, L. (n.d.). *A guide to SEA LIFE Orlando & tips for visiting.* Go City. https://gocity.com/orlando/en-us/blog/sea-life-aquarium-orlando-guide

Editors. (2023, February 17). *10 of the most beautiful hiking trails near Orlando.* OffMetro World. https://offmetro.com/world/31261/10-of-the-most-beautiful-hiking-trails-near-orlando/

Epcot food and wine festival 2023. (n.d.). WDWInfo. https://www.wdwinfo.com/disney-world/epcot/food-wine-festival.htm

Essential packing tips for visiting Orlando. (2015, September 25). Orlando Insider Vacations. https://orlandoinsidervacations.com/essential-packing-tips-for-visiting-orlando/

Eubanks, C. (2022, January 3). *What I learned on a trip to disney world with my 85-year-old grandmother.* Condé Nast Traveler. https://www.cntraveler.com/story/what-i-learned-on-a-trip-to-disney-world-with-my-85-year-old-grandmother

The Everglades. (2019). National Wildlife Federation. https://www.nwf.org/Educational-Resources/Wildlife-Guide/Wild-Places/Everglades

Everglades National Park. (n.d.). National Park Foundation. https://www.nationalparks.org/explore/parks/everglades-national-park

Everything you need to know about Aquatica Orlando. (n.d.). Undercover Tourist. https://www.undercovertourist.com/blog/aquatica-orlando-water-park/

Expert tips to make sure you get the best out of Orlando. (n.d.). Attraction Tickets. https://www.attractiontickets.com/en/latest-news/14-expert-tips-make-sure-you-get-best-out-orlando

Exploring hip and historic old town St. Augustine. (n.d.). TravlinMad. https://www.travlinmad.com/blog/old-town-st-augustine-attractions-florida

Fergusson, A. (2023, September 22). *25 top Orlando packing list items for 2023.* Asher & Lyric. https://www.asherfergusson.com/must-have-orlando-packing-list-items/

The 15 best bakeries in Orlando too good to keep secret. (2022, December 11). Westgate Resorts. https://www.westgateresorts.com/blog/bakeries-orlando/

15 restaurants on International Drive Orlando you have to try | I drive restaurants guide. (2019, March 22). WestgateResorts. https://www.westgateresorts.com/blog/15-restaurants-international-drive-orlando-you-have-to-try/

50+ romantic things to do in Orlando for couples. (2022, June 27). The Florida Travel Girl. https://thefloridatravelgirl.com/romantic-things-to-do-in-orlando/

Florida Department of Environmental Protection Greenways and Trails. (n.d.). *Wekiwa Springs State Park real Florida guide.* https://www.floridastateparks.org/sites/default/files/media/file/Wekiwa%20Springs%20Real%20Florida%20Guide.pdf

Florida trail tips and safety. (2017, January 4). Visit Florida. https://www.visitflorida.com/travel-ideas/articles/outdoors-nature-florida-trail-safety-tips/

Food and wine festivals. (n.d.). SeaWorld. https://seaworld.com/orlando/events/seven-seas-food-festival/

Food truck park: A foodies paradise. (n.d.). Food Truck Park Orlando. http://foodtruck-park.com/

Forstreuter, N. (2022, May 21). *Travel planning: 9 steps to set up the perfect itinerary.* Guide Your Travel. https://guideyourtravel.com/travel-planning-9-steps-to-set-up-the-perfect-itinerary/

40 fun Orlando facts. (2014, August 1). City of Orlando. http://www.cityoforlando.net/blog/40-fun-orlando-facts/

FOX 35 News Staff. (2023, April 16). *7 Orlando area restaurants with stunning waterfront views*. FOX 35 Orlando. https://www.fox35orlando.com/news/5-orlando-area-restaurants-with-incredible-waterfront-views

Fredrickson, R. (2023, September 2). *14 best rooftop bars in Orlando - complete guide*. The Rooftop Guide. https://www.therooftopguide.com/rooftop-bars-in-orlando.html

Fuhs, D. (2017, October 7). *Fun facts about Disney's monorail system*. Steps to Magic. https://stepstomagic.com/how-to-use-monorail/

Fun Spot America Orlando - Florida theme park guide. (n.d.). Villa Giant Florida. https://www.villagiant.com/theme-parks/fun-spot-america-orlando/

Fun Spot America: Orlando. (n.d.). https://www.getyourguide.com/orlando-l191/fun-spot-america-orlando-t431584/

Gatorland alligator park, Orlando, Forida. (n.d.). Orlando Attractions. https://www.orlandoattractions.com/orlando-attractions/distraction-attractions/gatorland/

Gayatri, S. (2021, April 20). *20 interesting facts about Orlando Florida (weird, geeky & fun!)*. Stories by Soumya. https://www.storiesbysoumya.com/facts-about-orlando-florida/

Gindin, R. (2023, January 23). *The 14 best neighborhoods in Orlando, Florida*. Landing.

https://www.hellolanding.com/blog/moving-guide-the-best-neighborhoods-in-orlando/

Glover, E. (2013, October 8). *The history of the Disneyland monorail: Mark I, 1959-1961*. Disney Parks Blog. https://disneyparks.disney.go.com/blog/2013/10/the-history-of-the-disneyland-monorail-mark-i-1959-1961/

Gotta Go Orlando. (2022, November 22). *The complete list of Orlando and Central Florida farmers markets*. Gotta Go Orlando. https://www.gottagoorlando.com/post/the-freshest-complete-list-of-central-florida-farmers-markets

GoWorld. (2023, January 3). *6 tips on how to get the best family holiday in Orlando, Florida*. Go World Travel Magazine. https://www.goworldtravel.com/family-holiday-in-orlando-florida/

Grant, A. (2022, April 23). *How much money to bring to Universal Studios? (5 costs to consider)*. Park Nerds. https://parknerds.com/money-to-bring-universal-studios/

Great ways to make new friends in Orlando. (2022, July 19). Unation. https://www.unation.com/stuff-to-do/great-ways-to-make-new-friends-in-orlando/

Gross, B. (2022, December 18). *Mount Dora: 12 things I love about this delightful town*. FloridaRambler. https://www.floridarambler.com/central-florida-getaways/mount-dora/

Gross, B. (2023a, January 15). *Best kayaking in Orlando and Central Florida: 15 wild rivers*. Florida Rambler. https://www.floridarambler.com/central-florida-getaways/kayaking-in-orlando/

Gross, B. (2023b, March 9). *11 nature parks in Orlando: Adventure beyond the theme parks.* Florida Rambler. https://www.floridarambler.com/kayaking-in-florida/nature-parks-in-orlando/

Guide to Wekiwa Springs State Park & Wekiva Island | Encore Resort. (2018, May 30). *Encore Resort at Reunion.* https://blog.encorereunion.com/guide-wekiwa-springs-wekiva-island/

Gurnani, S. (2021, December 2). *12 incredible places one must explore while on a day trip from Orlando!* Travel Triangle. https://traveltriangle.com/blog/day-trip-from-orlando/

Hall Mahon, S. (2023, March 4). *Mount Dora, Florida, is truly "someplace special."* Southern Living. https://www.southernliving.com/mount-dora-fl-7098627

Harris, L. (2023, February 18). *Date yourself first: 8 solo date ideas in Orlando.* Orlando Date Night Guide. https://www.orlandodatenightguide.com/2023/02/date-first-8-solo-date-ideas-orlando/

Harrison, C. (2023, September 11). *How much spending money to take to Orlando, Florida (2023).* Inside Our Suitcase. https://insideoursuitcase.com/how-much-spending-money-to-take-to-orlando/

Haunted or hoax: Seven spooky places in Orlando. (n.d.). Rosen Inn International. https://www.roseninn7600.com/blog/haunted-or-hoax-seven-spooky-places-in-orlando

Healey, K. (2018, February 6). *Safety tips: Hiking on Florida trails.* WFTV. https://www.wftv.com/news/local/safety-tips-hiking-on-florida-trails-/695285078/

The historic district in St. Augustine, FL. (n.d.). St Augustine Florida Vacation Guide. https://www.visitstaugustine.com/regions/historic-downtown

History in Orlando. (n.d.). Frommer's. https://www.frommers.com/destinations/orlando/in-depth/history

Holliday, P. (2023, September 4). *Your guide to using Uber Orlando and Lyft Orlando.* No-Guilt Life. https://noguiltlife.com/your-guide-to-using-uber-orlando-and-lyft-orlando/

Hot Air Balloon Festival. (n.d.). Visit Central Florida. https://visitcentralflorida.org/events/hot-air-balloon-festival/

How much money do you need for a week in Orlando Florida? (2023, October 2). Love the Maldives. https://lovethemaldives.com/faq/how-much-money-do-you-need-for-a-week-in-orlando-florida#

How to explore the Florida Everglades National Park. (n.d.). Visit Florida. https://www.visitflorida.com/things-to-do/outdoors-and-adventure/parks/everglades-national-park/

How to meet people in Orlando, Florida. (2018, June 3). Get the Friends You Want. https://getthefriendsyouwant.com/how-to-meet-people-in-orlando-florida/

Hussain, A. (2023, May 31). *The 12 best cheap hotels in Orlando, Florida.* UpgradedPoints. https://upgradedpoints.com/travel/hotels/best-cheap-hotels-in-orlando-florida/

Ideas for your family vacation in Orlando. (2021, March 2). Visit Florida. https://www.visitflorida.com/travel-ideas/articles/family-vacation-ideas-orlando/

Is Orlando safe for solo female travelers? Solo female travel safety index. (n.d.). Travelladies.app. https://travelladies.app/safety/united-states/orlando

J., N., & TPH Team. (2020, February 18). *9 safety tips for women traveling alone to Disney World (solo travel)*. ThemeParkHipster. https://www.themeparkhipster.com/safety-tips-for-women-traveling-alone-to-disney-world-2/

J., N., & TPH Team. (2023, April 13). *15 tips for planning a trip to Disney World on a budget (A guide for solo travelers)*. ThemeParkHipster. https://www.themeparkhipster.com/disney-world-on-a-budget-cheap-solo-travel/

Jones, I. (2022, July 30). *How to do Orlando on a budget*. Loveexploring.com. https://www.loveexploring.com/news/146985/orlando-on-a-budget-disney-world-florida-epcot-disney-parks

Katie. (2016, November 28). *30 top tips for visiting Orlando theme parks*. Creative Travel Guide. https://www.creativetravelguide.com/top-tips-for-visiting-orlando-theme-parks/

Kayaking spots in Orlando. (2022, January 25). OrlandoEscape. https://www.orlandoescape.com/kayaking-spots-in-orlando/

Kerry. (2022, February 7). *Best things to do in Orlando alone + pros/cons of going solo*. Vegg Travel. https://veggtravel.com/things-to-do-in-orlando-alone/

Ketcham, S. (2018, February 10). *7 Central Florida museums where kids can play - and learn*. Visit Florida. https://www.visitflorida.com/travel-ideas/articles/arts-history-children-museums-orlando-central-florida/

Laura. (2021, December 29). *Where to walk in Orlando*. Orlando on the Cheap. https://orlandoonthecheap.com/walking-paths-orlando/

Leap. (2023a, March 8). *Tips to maximize your time at Walt Disney World*. Undercover Tourist. https://www.undercovertourist.com/blog/maximize-your-time-walt-disney-world/

Leap. (2023b, July 11). *Our galactic guide to Kennedy Space Center*. Undercover Tourist. https://www.undercovertourist.com/blog/guide-kennedy-space-center/

Leap. (2023c, September 6). *Our frog family guide to Orlando transportation outside the resorts*. Undercover Tourist. https://www.undercovertourist.com/blog/orlando-transportation/

LEGOLAND Florida | Guide to attractions, shows, & tickets. (n.d.). Visit Orlando. https://www.visitorlando.com/things-to-do/theme-parks/legoland-florida-resort/legoland-florida-theme-park/

LEGOLAND Florida Resort | Theme park guide, tickets & info. (n.d.). Visit Orlando. https://www.visitorlando.com/things-to-do/theme-parks/legoland-florida-resort/

Luberecki, B. (2023, August 24). *The 10 best hotels in Orlando*. Forbes. https://www.forbes.com/sites/forbes-personal-shopper/2023/08/24/best-hotels-in-orlando/?sh=369669944857

Lukaszewicz, H. (2023, January 17). *Top 10 tasty cheap eats at Universal Orlando.* Getting Stamped. https://www.gettingstamped.com/cheap-eats-at-universal-orlando/

Ly, R. (2014, April 17). *10 bizarre foods Andrew Zimmern might like in orlando.* Tasty Chomps: A Local's Culinary Guide. https://tastychomps.com/2014/04/andrew-zimmerns-bizarre-foods-in-orlando-florida.html

Make it an overnight. Orlando resorts made for romance. (2021, December 15). 10Best. https://10best.usatoday.com/destinations/florida/orlando/hotels/romantic-hotels/

Make the most out of your Universal Orlando Resort adventure. (n.d.). Universal Orlando Resort. https://www.universalorlando.com/web/en/us/plan-your-visit/prepare-for-your-visit

Manieri, K. (2023, October 17). *Our favorite Orlando seafood restaurants for (sea)foodies.* Orlando Date Night Guide. https://www.orlandodatenightguide.com/2023/04/orlando-seafood-restaurants/

Mansurov, N. (2010, June 28). *Florida birding near Orlando.* Photography Life. https://photographylife.com/florida-birding-near-orlando

Mariah, R. (2022, August 29). *The top 10 best Disney restaurants on a budget at Walt Disney World.* Polka Dots and Pixie Dust. https://www.polkadotsandpixiedust.com/best-disney-restaurants-on-a-budget/

Mayntz, M. (2022, October 15). *30 best birds to see in Florida.* The Spruce. https://www.thespruce.com/florida-bird-species-4582420

McKechnie, G. (2019, December 6). *Wekiwa springs state park: Orlando's main spring.* Visit Florida. https://www.visitflorida.com/travel-ideas/articles/outdoors-nature-wekiwa-springs/

Orlando announces 74 million visitors in 2022, ranking as no. 1 U.S. travel destination. (2023, May 11). Visit Orlando. https://www.visitorlando.com/media/press-releases/post/orlando-announces-74-million-visitors-in-2022-ranking-as-no-1-us-travel-destination

Melissa. (2023a, January 19). *25 essential tips for Universal Studios Orlando.* The Family Voyage. https://www.thefamilyvoyage.com/tips-for-universal-studios-orlando/

Melissa. (2023b, October 9). *25 tips for Disney World that won't make you crazy.* The Family Voyage. https://www.thefamilyvoyage.com/tips-for-disney-world-first-time/

Meyering, D. (2023a, January 9). *A beer lover's guide to Orlando breweries for date night.* Orlando Date Night Guide. https://www.orlandodatenightguide.com/2023/01/orlando-breweries/

Meyering, D. (2023b, August 21). *15 scenic waterfront restaurants Orlando - around town and nearby.* Orlando Date Night Guide. https://www.orlandodatenightguide.com/2023/08/waterfront-restaurants/

Meyering, D. (2023c, October 1). *The tastiest fall foodie events in Orlando 2023.* Orlando Date Night Guide.

https://www.orlandodatenightguide.com/2023/10/fall-foodie-food-events-orlando/

Michaela. (2023, February 7). *Tips for seaworld orlando - an insider's guide to the park*. Tripster Travel Guide. https://www.tripster.com/travelguide/seaworld-facts-know/

Mickle, N. (2022, September 20). *87 epic things to do in Orlando*. Florida Homes and Living. https://floridahomesandliving.com/things-to-do-in-orlando-florida/

Miller, J., & Miller, R. (2023, May 12). *Your complete guide to Wekiwa Springs*. Getaway Couple. https://www.getawaycouple.com/wekiwa-springs/

Miller, M. (2023, July 1). *The history of Orlando and how it was named*. Florida Back Roads Travel. https://www.florida-backroads-travel.com/history-of-orlando.html

Mini golf in Orlando. (2023). Tripadvisor. https://www.tripadvisor.com/Attractions-g34515-Activities-c56-t271-Orlando_Florida.html

Mommy Frog. (2023a, February 16). *The best food and drink items at Universal Orlando Resort*. Undecover Tourist. https://www.undercovertourist.com/blog/best-food-universal-orlando/

Mommy Frog. (2023b, May 23). *Disney World weather (and how to pack for it!)*. Undercover Tourist. https://www.undercovertourist.com/blog/how-to-pack-for-orlando-theme-parks/

Mommy Frog. (2023c, May 30). *Eating at Disney World on a budget*. Undercover Tourist.

https://www.undercovertourist.com/blog/eating-at-disney-world-on-a-budget/

Mommy Frog. (2023d, August 10). *The best theme parks in Orlando by age group*. Undercover Tourist. https://www.undercovertourist.com/blog/the-best-orlando-theme-parks-by-age-group/

Mommy Frog. (2023e, September 10). *Our top spots for cheap food at Disney World*. Undercover Tourist. https://www.undercovertourist.com/blog/cheap-food-at-disney-world/

Mommy Frog. (2023f, October 17). *Our top tips for eating on a budget at Universal Orlando*. WUndercover Tourist. https://www.undercovertourist.com/blog/eating-on-a-budget-universal-orlando/

Monzon, R. (2023, May 30). *The ultimate guide to Walt Disney World Resort in Florida for a magical time*. Klook Travel Blog. https://www.klook.com/blog/walt-disney-world-florida/

Most romantic hotels for couples in Orlando 2023. (2023). Hotels with Hot Tub in Room. https://hotelswithhottubinroom.club/florida/romantic-hotels-in-orlando/

National Park Service. (2017). *Everglades National Park (U.S. National Park Service)*. National Park Service. https://www.nps.gov/ever/index.htm

Neufeid, K. (2022, June 30). *15 epic day trips from Orlando for 2023 (by a local!)*. Travel Lemming. https://travellemming.com/day-trips-from-orlando/

Neufeid, K. (2023, July 5). *21 things to do in Orlando for kids (by a local mom)*. Travel Lemming.

https://travellemming.com/things-to-do-in-orlando-with-kids/

Neufeld, K. (2023a, March 16). *Kennedy Space Center*. Travel Lemmingm. https://travellemming.com/kennedy-space-center/

Neufeld, K. (2023b, July 3). *The best time to visit Orlando? When to go, by a local*. Travel Lemming. https://travellemming.com/best-time-to-visit-orlando/

Neufeld, K. (2023c, July 5). *34 best things to do in Orlando in 2023 (by a local)*. Travel Lemming. https://travellemming.com/things-to-do-in-orlando/

Neufeld, K. (2023d, July 5). *Where to stay in Orlando, by an area local*. Travel Lemming. https://travellemming.com/where-to-stay-in-orlando/

Neufied, K. (2021, October 6). *Orlando on a budget - how to eat, stay, & do it cheaply*. Travel Lemming. https://travellemming.com/orlando-on-a-budget/

Nieminen, S. (2021, January 27). *My 20 most romantic hotels in Orlando*. Romantichotels.guide. https://romantichotels.guide/orlando/

NikkyJ. (2023, June 27). *Top 5 cheapest, best food at Universal Studios under $10*. ThemeParkHipster. https://www.themeparkhipster.com/cheapest-best-food-at-universal-studios/

9 swoonworthy romantic hotels in Orlando. (2020, June 16). Coleman Concierge. https://www.colemanconcierge.com/romantic-hotels-orlando/

19 incredibly romantic things to do in Orlando. (2020, May 2). Coleman Concierge. https://www.colemanconcierge.com/romantic-things-to-do-in-orlando/

Nissman, I. M. (2022, June 17). *Packing list for Orlando*. Tripster Travel Guide. https://www.tripster.com/travelguide/what-to-bring-to-orlando/

Nissman, I. M. (2023, January 9). *Romantic restaurants in Orlando: 15 best date night dining options*. Tripster Travel Guide. https://www.tripster.com/travelguide/13-most-romantic-restaurants-in-orlando/

Ocala National Forest Things to do for VIEWS! camping, hiking, picnic, swimming, turtles, alligators Florida travel blog. (n.d.). Flashpacking America. https://www.flashpackingamerica.com/florida-travel/things-to-do-in-ocala-national-forest/

Orlando 2019: Best of Orlando, FL tourism. (2019). TripAdvisor. https://www.tripadvisor.com/Tourism-g34515-Orlando_Florida-Vacations.html

Orlando activities | rides and go karts | skycoaster. (n.d.). Fun Spot America. https://fun-spot.com/orlando/

Orlando animal encounters and tours. (n.d.). SeaWorld Orlando. https://seaworld.com/orlando/tours/

Orlando animal experiences & interactive tours. (2020). SeaWorld Orlando. https://seaworld.com/orlando/animal-experiences/

Orlando boat tours. (n.d.). Travelocity. https://www.travelocity.com/discover/united-states-of-america/florida/orlando.d178294/things-to-do/boat-tours

Orlando breweries. (n.d.). Visit Orlando. https://www.visitorlando.com/things-to-do/eat-drink/breweries/

Orlando dining. (n.d.). International Drive Orlando. https://www.internationaldriveorlando.com/things-to-do/orlando-dining/

Orlando events calendar. (n.d.). Visit Orlando. https://www.orlandomeeting.com/explore/events/

Orlando events calendar | find concerts, festivals & exhibits. (2023). Visit Orlando. https://www.visitorlando.com/events/

Orlando Festivals | Film, Arts, Music, Food & Cultural Events. (2023). Visit Orlando. Visit Orlando

Orlando, FL Festivals. (2023). Eventbrite. https://www.eventbrite.com/d/fl--orlando/festivals/

Orlando, Florida. (2023, October 21). In *Wikipedia.* https://en.wikipedia.org/w/index.php?title=Orlando,_Florida&oldid=1187178701

Orlando food trucks. (n.d.). Roaminghunger.com. https://roaminghunger.com/food-trucks/orlando-fl/1/

Orlando history. (2019). City of Orlando. https://www.orlando.gov/Our-Government/History

Orlando Lake Butler tours. (n.d.). Orlando Lake Tours. https://www.orlandolaketours.com/

Orlando museums & galleries. (n.d.). Hotels.com Phillipenes. https://ph.hotels.com/go/usa/orlando-museums-galleries

Orlando park hours. (2015). Fun Spot America. https://fun-spot.com/

Orlando theme park tips & tricks to save your sanity. (2016, December 15). Orlando Insider Vacations. https://orlandoinsidervacations.com/orlando-theme-park-tips/

Orlando Transportation. (n.d.). Visit Orlando. https://www.visitorlando.com/plan/transportation/?view=list&sort=qualityScore

Orlando travel costs. (2016, November 7). Budget Your Trip. https://www.budgetyourtrip.com/united-states-of-america/orlando

Orlando weather. (n.d.). Hotels.com Phillipines. https://ph.hotels.com/go/usa/orlando-weather

Orlando weather | find forecast, averages & climate. (n.d.). Visit Orlando. https://www.visitorlando.com/plan/weather/

Orlando's international drive entertainment district. (n.d.). Visit Orlando. https://www.visitorlando.com/things-to-do/more-things-to-do/international-drive/

Our expert guide to dining on a budget in orlando. (n.d.). Attraction Tickets. https://www.attractiontickets.com/en/latest-news/orlando/attractionticketscoms-expert-guide-dining-budget-orlando

Orlando Weekly Staff. (2023, March 9). *Wild day-trip destinations near Orlando*. Orlando Weekly.

https://www.orlandoweekly.com/orlando/wild-day-trip-destinations-near-orlando/Slideshow/33681339

Orlando Weekly Staff. (2021, July 30). *20 classic Orlando dive bars everyone should visit at least once.* Orlando Weekly. https://www.orlandoweekly.com/orlando/20-classic-orlando-dive-bars-everyone-should-visit-at-least-once/Slideshow/30946519/30725078

Parker, E. (2021, June 28). *Tips for visiting SeaWorld Orlando - SeaWorld travel guide.* The Journey of Parenthood... https://www.journeyofparenthood.com/tips-for-visiting-seaworld-orlando-seaworld-travel-guide/

Patterson, S. (2023a, June 22). *5 Central Florida kayaking experiences every Orlandoan needs to have.* Orlando Date Night Guide. https://www.orlandodatenightguide.com/2023/06/central-florida-kayaking/

Patterson, S. (2023b, July 30). *Orlando's most romantic experiences.* Orlando Date Night Guide. https://www.orlandodatenightguide.com/most-romantic-experiences-in-orlando/

Patterson, S. (2023c, October 11). *Orlando's Most Romantic Restaurants.* Orlando Date Night Guide. https://www.orlandodatenightguide.com/2023/04/orlandos-most-romantic-restaurants-2/

Pattiz, T. (2023, October 4). *9 BEST national parks near Orlando (guide + photos).* More than Just Parks | National Parks Guides. https://morethanjustparks.com/national-parks-near-orlando/

Pelling, K. (2016, December 11). *10 unusual things to do in Orlando besides Disney.* Family Adventure Project.

https://www.familyadventureproject.org/10-unusual-things-to-do-in-orlando/

Pevehouse, B. (2022, May 18). *10 hiking trails in Orlando worth the journey.* FloridaIsHome.com. https://www.floridaishome.com/blog/10-hiking-trails-in-orlando-worth-the-journey/

Pinto, A. (2019, August 16). *Top 15 bed & breakfasts in Orlando.* Bed-And-Breakfast.me. https://bed-and-breakfast.me/orlando/

Places to stay in orlando. (n.d.). Visit Orlando. https://www.visitorlando.com/places-to-stay/?view=list&sort=qualityScore

Plan your visit to LEGOLAND Florida resort. (n.d.). LEGOLAND Florida Resort. https://www.legoland.com/florida/plan-your-visit/

Public Transit. (n.d.). City of Orlando. https://www.orlando.gov/Parking-Transportation/Public-Transit

R., E. (2023, August 22). *Beat the heat: The ultimate guide to staying cool at SeaWorld Orlando.* Seaworld.com. https://seaworld.com/orlando/blog/keep-cool-at-seaworld-orlando/

Rajguru, R. (2022, September 24). *How to make conversations with locals while traveling.* Turuhi. https://turuhi.com/resources/how-to-make-conversations-with-locals-while-traveling/

Ransome, S. (2023, June 2). *Top 10 art museums in Orlando, Florida.* ART by SARAH RANSOME. https://www.sarahransomeart.com/blog/top-art-museums-in-orlando-florida

Rattenbury, J. (2023a, June 1). *11 fantastic bakeries in Orlando with the best pastries.* Secret Orlando. https://secretorlando.co/bakeries-orlando/

Rattenbury, J. (2023b, July 12). *9 seafood restaurants in Orlando that are an absolute catch!* Secret Orlando. https://secretorlando.co/seafood-restaurants-orlando/

Real Coast to Coast. (2022, September 24). *The Villages Florida | Tour the #1 Retirement community in the world.* YouTube. https://www.youtube.com/watch?v=GOSh0B9tphI

Rebecca and Jonathan. (n.d.). *Rebecca & Jonathan share their Orlando holiday story.* American Sky. https://www.americansky.co.uk/florida-holidays/orlando/rebecca-jonathan-share-their-orlando-holiday-story

Reeve, D. (2023, January 24). *Best mini golf in Orlando: 12 top putt putt places! (2023).* Family Destinations Guide/. https://familydestinationsguide.com/best-mini-golf-in-orlando-fl/

Rhodes, E. (2022, December 8). *40 Disney World foods everyone should try at least once.* Travel + Leisure. https://www.travelandleisure.com/trip-ideas/disney-vacations/best-disney-world-food

Ricky. (2019, July 8). *26 great things to pack for Orlando Florida that you haven't thought of.* World Travel Toucan. https://worldtraveltoucan.com/things-to-pack-for-your-orlando-florida-holiday/

Rodgers, G. (2021, April 19). *10 essential safety tips all hikers should follow.* TripSavvy. https://www.tripsavvy.com/essential-safety-tips-for-every-hike-5176614

Rodriguez Flores, E., & Simonson, J. (2023, June 16). *What to pack for Orlando.* KAYAK. https://www.kayak.co.uk/Orlando.9900.guide/what-to-pack-orlando

Rosenthal, S. (2023, October 21). *A guide to Orlando farmers markets.* Orlando Date Night Guide. https://www.orlandodatenightguide.com/2023/07/guide-to-orlando-farmers-markets/

Rotondo, A. M. (2022, September 6). *TPG's complete guide to Universal Orlando.* The Points Guy. https://thepointsguy.com/guide/universal-orlando/

Rountree, B. (2017, September 21). *6 things to do in Ocala National Forest.* Florida Rambler. https://www.floridarambler.com/kayaking-in-florida/things-to-do-ocala-national-forest/

Roy, A. (2021, December 3). *7 best zoos in Orlando to treat the kid inside you like never before!* Travel Triangle. https://traveltriangle.com/blog/zoos-in-orlando/

Scott. (2022, April 11). *Here's where to go BIRD WATCHING near Disney World (& Orlando).* Bird Watching HQ. https://birdwatchinghq.com/bird-watching-near-disney-world/

Scott, C. (2023, February 5). *A guide to Orlando museums of art.* See Great Art. https://www.seegreatart.art/a-guide-to-orlando-museums-of-art/

SEA LIFE. (2019). *SEA LIFE Orlando aquarium | ICON park attraction.* Visit Sea Life. https://www.visitsealife.com/orlando/

SeaWorld Orlando | theme park guide, tips & tickets info. (n.d.). Visit Orlando. https://www.visitorlando.com/things-to-do/theme-parks/seaworld-orlando/seaworld/

7 travel tips visiting Orlando Florida. (2021, August 18). Real Florida Adventures. https://realfloridaadventures.com/7-travel-tips-visiting-orlando-florida/

17 easy day trips from Orlando perfect for nature lovers. (2020, December 6). Travlinmad. https://www.travlinmad.com/blog/day-trips-from-orlando

Shelton, N. (2022, April 11). *Walk on the wild side at Orlando zoos and gardens.* Visit Orlando. https://www.visitorlando.com/blog/post/orlando-zoos-gardens/

Shelton, N. (2023, July 31). *Dig into Orlando's fantastic fall foodie festivals.* Visit Orlando. https://www.visitorlando.com/blog/post/fall-food-festivals-orlando/

Site Staff. (2023, May 13). *15 intriguing day trips from Orlando you wouldn't want to miss.* TripMemos. https://tripmemos.com/day-trips-orlando-florida/

Six best annual festivals in Orlando to attend. (2017, December 15). Hotel Escape. https://www.hotelsescape.com/six-best-annual-festivals-in-orlando-to-attend/

16 best international drive restaurants: Places to eat on i-drive. (2022, February 2). Hey! East Coast USA. https://heyeastcoastusa.com/best-international-drive-restaurants/

16 cool and unusual things to do in Orlando. (2023, June 15). Atlas Obscura. https://www.atlasobscura.com/things-to-do/orlando-florida

Spears, S. (2023, May 2). *11 unusual things to do in Orlando.* Florida Travel Life. https://www.floridatravellife.com/florida-spotlight/weird-things-to-do-in-orlando-florida/

Spitzer, M. (2022, August 13). *Orlando's best seafood joints will have you hooked.* 10Best. https://10best.usatoday.com/destinations/florida/orlando/restaurants/seafood/

St Cloud Florida - things to do & attractions in St Cloud FL. (2020, March 25). Visit Florida. https://www.visitflorida.com/places-to-go/central/st-cloud/

Stuart Pratt, M. (2023, April 1). *Ultimate guide to Disney World for 2023 → Let the fun begin!* Miss Tourist. https://misstourist.com/guide-to-disney-world-florida-usa/

Tad. (2023, August 7). *The awesome insider's guide to LEGOLAND Florida.* Undercover Tourist. https://www.undercovertourist.com/blog/insiders-guide-legoland-florida/

Taracatac, J. (2020, August 5). *Moving to Orlando: A guide to downtown Orlando neighborhoods.* Megan's Moving. https://megansmoving.com/moving-to-orlando-a-guide-to-downtown-orlando-neighborhoods/

Taylor, B. (2023, March 14). *Solo travel: Tips for traveling to Universal Orlando alone.* Explore. https://www.explore.com/1226269/solo-travel-tips-for-traveling-to-universal-orlando-alone/

Taylor, R. (2021, June 24). *5 nature-filled day trips from Orlando.* Holiday Inn Club. https://holidayinnclub.com/blog/nature-day-trips-from-orlando

The 10 best budget hotels in orlando,. (n.d.). Booking.com. https://www.booking.com/budget/city/us/orlando.en-gb.html?

The 10 best cheap hotels in Orlando 2023 (with prices). (n.d.). Trip Advisor. Retrieved October 22, 2023, from https://www.tripadvisor.com/HotelsList-Orlando-Cheap-Hotels-zfp10315.html

10 dessert places in Orlando to die for! (2020, April 21). Westgate Resorts. https://www.westgateresorts.com/blog/10-dessert-places-orlando/

10 fun facts about Orlando. (2017, July 26). WorldStrides. https://worldstrides.com/blog/2017/07/10-fun-facts-orlando/

10 intriguing things in the St. Augustine historic district. (2020, August 22). St. Francis Inn. https://stfrancisinn.com/blog/explore-the-st-augustine-historic-district/

10 must-visit speakeasies in orlando. (2023, August 28). Unation. https://www.unation.com/stuff-to-do/our-favorite-speakeasies-in-orlando/

10 of the best family dinner shows in Orlando. (2022, November 30). Mango's Tropical Cafe. https://mangos.com/orlando/10-of-the-best-family-dinner-shows-in-orlando/

10 things to know for your first time in Orlando. (n.d.). Hotels.com Phillipenes. https://ph.hotels.com/go/usa/orlando-first-time-trip-tips

10 tips for travelling in Orlando with children. (n.d.). Hotels.com Phillipenes. https://ph.hotels.com/go/usa/orlando-children-travel-tips

The 20 best food trucks Orlando locals lunch at! (2021, November 9). WestgateResorts. https://www.westgateresorts.com/blog/20-food-trucks-orlando/

The 25 romantic Orlando restaurants for date night in 2023 - the florida travel girl. (2023, January 22). The Florida Travel Girl. https://thefloridatravelgirl.com/romantic-orlando-restaurants/

The Editors of Encyclopedia Britannica. (2023a, October 4). Everglades | region, Florida, United States. In *Encyclopedia Britannica.* https://www.britannica.com/place/Everglades

The Editors of Encyclopedia Britannica. (2023b, October 22). Orlando | history, attractions, & facts. In *Encyclopedia Britannica.* https://www.britannica.com/place/Orlando-Florida

The top 5 Orlando festivals & cultural events. (n.d.). Tripadvisor. https://www.tripadvisor.ie/Attractions-g34515-Activities-c62-t282-Orlando_Florida.html

The top 10 Orlando cultural tours (w/prices). (n.d.). Viator. https://www.viator.com/en-PH/Orlando-tours/Cultural-and-Theme-Tours/d663-g4

The top 10 Orlando transportation services (w/prices). (n.d.). Viator. https://www.viator.com/Orlando-tours/Airport-Services/d663-g15-c54

The Villages travel guide 2023 - things to do, what to eat & tips. (n.d.). Trip.com. Retrieved October 23, 2023, from https://www.trip.com/travel-guide/destination/the-villages-38295/

Theme Park Center. (2023, February 1). *17 tips for Visiting Gatorland Orlando | explained*. Theme Park Center. https://themeparkcenter.com/blogs/mice-magic-the-official-theme-park-center-blog/7-things-to-know-before-going-to-gatorland-2019-w-pictures

Things to do alone in Orlando. (2022, October 24). Girl about the Globe. https://www.girlabouttheglobe.com/things-to-do-alone-in-orlando/

Things to do in Orlando's neighborhoods & nearby cities. (n.d.). Visit Orlando. https://www.visitorlando.com/things-to-do/more-things-to-do/neighborhoods/

13 best restaurants for waterfront dining in Orlando. (2023, March 10). Unation. https://www.unation.com/stuff-to-do/waterfront-dining-in-orlando/

31 affordable places to eat around Orlando. (2023, March 19). LemonHearted. https://www.lemonhearted.com/blog/cheap-orlando-eats-under-15

This isn't a fairytale vacation. This isn't make believe. This is as real as it gets. (n.d.). Universal Orlando Resort. https://www.universalorlando.com/web/en/us/plan-your-visit/theme-park-first-time-guide

Thomas, E. (2023, September 21). *Best rooftop bars & restaurants in Orlando*. Orlando Date Night Guide. https://www.orlandodatenightguide.com/2023/09/best-rooftop-bars-restaurants-in-orlando/

Tips & tricks for visiting Orlando with small kids. (n.d.). Visit Orlando. https://www.visitorlando.com/things-to-do/things-to-do-with-kids/top-tips-and-tricks-orlando-with-small-kids/

Tips for solo travelers to Orlando. (2022, September 27). OrlandoEscape. https://www.orlandoescape.com/tips-for-solo-travelers-to-orlando/

Todd, C. L. (2019, May 10). *14 essential safety tips to follow before and during every hike*. SELF. https://www.self.com/story/hiking-safety-tips

Top 7 tips for solo travel in Orlando, Florida. (2022, December 29). Rosen Plaza. https://www.rosenplaza.com/solo-travel-orlando/

Top 9 most romantic things to do in Orlando. (n.d.). Holiday Inn Club. https://holidayinnclub.com/blog/romantic-things-to-do-in-orlando

Top 10 animal encounters in Orlando. (2018, November 7). Attraction Tickets. https://www.attractiontickets.com/en/latest-news/orlando/seaworldr-orlando-tickets/top-10-animal-encounters-orlando

Top 10 best bakeries near Orlando, Florida. (2023). Yelp. https://www.yelp.com/search?cflt=bakeries&find_loc=Orlando%2C+FL

Top 10 best boat tours in Orlando, FL. (2023, October). Yelp. https://www.yelp.com/search?find_desc=Boat+Tours&find_loc=Orlando%2C+FL

Top 10 Best Cuban Food in Orlando, FL. (2023, October). Yelp. https://www.yelp.com/search?find_desc=Cuban+Food&find_loc=Orlando%2C+FL

Top 10 Best Romantic Restaurants With a View in Orlando, FL. (2023). Yelp. https://www.yelp.com/search?find_desc=Romantic+Restaurants+With+A+View&find_loc=Orlando%2C+FL

Travel Pedia. (10 C.E., January). *How much money do you need per day in Orlando?* Love the Maldives. https://lovethemaldives.com/faq/how-much-money-do-you-need-per-day-in-orlando

Travel Pedia. (2023, September 30). *Is Orlando the most visited city?* Love the Maldives. https://lovethemaldives.com/faq/is-orlando-the-most-visited-city#

Travel, K. (2023, March 15). *What to expect and what to do in SEA LIFE Orlando aquarium*. Klook Travel Blog. https://www.klook.com/blog/to-do-sea-life-orlando/

Travis. (2023, July 12). *29 romantic things to do in orlando: Fun date ideas & special romantic celebration options*. Hey! East Coast USA. https://heyeastcoastusa.com/romantic-things-to-do-in-orlando/

Turner, K. (2019, January 25). *10+ interesting day trips from Orlando for nature and culture lovers*. Wanderlustingk. https://www.wanderlustingk.com/travel-blog/day-trips-orlando-nature-culture

12 best hikes in Orlando you shouldn't miss. (2021, July 18). Florida Trippers. https://floridatrippers.com/best-hikes-in-orlando/

29 Incredible Universal Orlando tips [SAVE MONEY & TIME]. (2023, April 28). Globalmunchkins.com. https://globalmunchkins.com/destinations/theme-parks/universal-orlando/the-best-universal-orlando-tips-from-a-pro/

2023 best romantic restaurants Orlando. (2023). Gayot. https://www.gayot.com/restaurants/best-orlando-fl-top10-romanticrestaurant_19or.html

2023 EPCOT food and wine festival. (2022, November 20). The Disney Food Blog. https://www.disneyfoodblog.com/2023-epcot-food-and-wine-festival/

2023 guide to Epcot food & wine festival. (2023, September 1). Mouse Hacking. https://www.mousehacking.com/blog/epcot-international-food-and-wine-festival

The ultimate guide to planning a Walt Disney World vacation. (2021, April 22). The Disney Food Blog. https://www.disneyfoodblog.com/the-ultimate-guide-to-planning-a-walt-disney-world-vacation/

The ultimate guide to Walt Disney World food. (2018, December 27). The Disney Food Blog. https://www.disneyfoodblog.com/the-ultimate-guide-to-walt-disney-world-food/

The ultimate guide: Planning your family visit to the Kennedy Space Center. (n.d.). Vacation Central Florida. https://www.vacationcentralflorida.com/blog/ultimate-guide-planning-your-family-visit-kennedy-space-center

Universal Orlando trip planning guide. (2023, January 15). Mouse Hacking. https://www.mousehacking.com/blog/universal-orlando-trip-planning-guide

Victoria. (2023, October 20). *10 unmissable things to do in Orlando with kids.* Bridges and Balloons. https://bridgesandballoons.com/things-to-do-in-orlando-with-kids/

Vierow, D. (2019, July 6). *Planning a travel itinerary: The complete guide.* Plan, Ready, Go. https://planreadygo.com/planning-a-travel-itinerary/

Walker, M. (2023, June 6). *Museums for kids in Orlando.* Orlando Family Fun Magazine. https://orlandofamilyfunmag.com/museums-for-kids-in-orlando/

Walking Tours. (n.d.). Saint Cloud Main Street. https://stcloudmainstreet.org/walking-tours/

Walt Disney World planning guide (2023 & 2024). (2023, September 13). Mouse Hacking. https://www.mousehacking.com/blog/walt-disney-world-planning-guide

waynekask. (2023, March 8). *Is Orlando safe? Everything to know before visiting in 2023!* ALWAYS on the SHORE. https://alwaysontheshore.com/is-orlando-safe/

Wekiwa Springs State Park. (n.d.-a). Florida State Parks. https://www.floridastateparks.org/parks-and-trails/wekiwa-springs-state-park

Wekiwa Springs State Park. (n.d.-b). Tripadvisor. https://www.tripadvisor.com/Attraction_Review-g29171-d145739-Reviews-Wekiwa_Springs_State_Park-Apopka_Florida.html

Wekiwa Springs State Park. (n.d.-c). Canoe Wekiva. , from https://www.canoewekiva.com/

Westgate Resorts. (2023, June 19). *20 fun facts about Orlando Florida you probably never knew*. WestgateResorts. https://www.westgateresorts.com/blog/orlando-fun-facts/

What to pack for an Orlando trip. (n.d.). Gotta Go Orlando. https://www.gottagoorlando.com/what-to-pack-for-florida

Which is better to use in Orlando Uber or Lyft? (n.d.). Love the Maldives. R https://lovethemaldives.com/faq/which-is-better-to-use-in-orlando-uber-or-lyft

Wisel, C. (2019, September 27). *The 22 best things to eat at Universal Orlando Resort*. Eater. https://www.eater.com/maps/best-restaurants-things-to-eat-universal-orlando-resort

Woodruff, M., & Woodruff, D. (2023, June 21). *Best Orlando boat tours*. Sometimes Home: Couples Travel. https://sometimeshome.com/orlando-boat-tours/

World food trucks. (n.d.). World Food Trucks. https://www.worldfoodtrucks.com/

World Strides. (2017, July 26). *10 fun facts about Orlando*. WorldStrides. https://worldstrides.com/blog/2017/07/10-fun-facts-orlando/

Zrallack, B. (2019, October 29). *Zoo and animal guide for Central Florida*. MyCentralFloridaFamily.com.

https://mycentralfloridafamily.com/zoo-and-animal-guide/

Image References

Adderley, C. (2019). *Photo of castle during daytime* [Image]. Pexels. https://www.pexels.com/photo/photo-of-castle-during-daytime-3411135/

Bergmann, M. (2021). *Orange and white fish on ice* [Image]. Unsplash. https://unsplash.com/photos/orange-and-white-fish-on-white-and-black-pebbles-tHjXXy1kk_QImage

Dias, M. (2019). *Fun town signage at LEGOLAND* [Image]. Unsplash. https://unsplash.com/photos/fun-town-signage-in-front-of-building-HIeRPh3JcwoImage

Dumlao, N. (2017). *Couple facing city* [Image]. Unsplash. https://unsplash.com/photos/couple-sitting-on-the-field-facing-the-city-EdULZpOKsUEImage

EL Evangelista. (2016). *ICON wheel at night* [Image]. Pexels. https://www.pexels.com/photo/ferris-wheel-during-night-time-1060901/Image

Ferrer, R. (2018). *Alligator on body of water* [Image]. *Pexels*. https://www.pexels.com/photo/alligator-near-water-plant-on-body-of-water-1360123/Image

Gallian, S. (2022). *Cocoa beach sunrise* [Image]. Unsplash. https://unsplash.com/photos/an-aerial-view-of-a-beach-and-ocean-at-sunset-B7nsKUoqHu8Image

Grootes, M. (2017). *Brown hat photo* [Image]. Unsplash. https://unsplash.com/photos/brown-hat-TVllFyGaLEAImage

Haupt, M. (2021). *A lovely day at my favorite local botanical garden* [Image]. Unsplash. https://unsplash.com/photos/a-woman-and-child-walking-down-a-path-in-the-woods-vOZF5BzUtqQImage

Jarritos Mexican Soda. (2021). *Woman in white and blue drinking jaritos* [Image]. Unsplash. https://unsplash.com/photos/woman-in-white-and-blue-floral-tank-top-holding-yellow-plastic-cup-MK0ispKjJv4Image

Kagels, R. T. (2023). *About the author* [Image]

Kalebe, A. (2023). *A street with cars parked* [Image]. Unsplash. https://unsplash.com/photos/a-street-with-cars-parked-on-the-side-of-it-L76-rKi9QKoImage

Madrigal, D. (2020). *Grey feather bird on brown wooden stick* [Image]. Pexels. https://www.pexels.com/photo/grey-feather-bird-on-brown-wooden-stick-3660658/Image

McGowan, B. (2020). *EPCOT international flower and garden festival* (2020) [Computer Rendering]. Unsplash.

Mewes, N. (2021). *A map with a pair of gasses* [Image]. Unsplash. https://unsplash.com/photos/a-map-with-a-pair-of-glasses-on-top-of-it-vANOIabNFR4Image

Milenkovic, D. (n.d.). *A city street at night with buildings* [Image]. Unsplash. https://unsplash.com/photos/a-city-street-at-night-with-buildings-lit-up-DrhFrjxrQpcImage

NASA. (2021). *Space shuttle Columbia* [Image]. Unsplash. https://unsplash.com/photos/space-shuttle-columbia-launches-from-the-kennedy-space-center-084iI8XTfN0Image

Petsos, C. (2022). *Mel's drive-in restaurant* [Image]. Pexels. https://www.pexels.com/photo/mels-drive-in-restaurant-at-universal-studios-orlando-florida-usa-14017467/Image

Stalin, J. (2021). *People with black and white whale* [Image]. Unsplash. https://unsplash.com/photos/people-in-black-and-white-whale-in-the-middle-of-the-sea-during-daytime-l6MuQo_X6xoImage

Taha. (2022). *Two people (Mickey and Minnie) in clothing* [Image]. Unsplash. https://unsplash.com/photos/two-people-in-clothing-a4p8FMIJ0JcImage

Vyas, A. (2021). *Blue and white globe at Universal Studios* [Image]. Unsplash. https://unsplash.com/photos/blue-and-white-globe-near-body-of-water-during-daytime-HCKVHAEbkusImage

Printed in Great Britain
by Amazon